COOKING
A BASIC REPERTOIRE

Erleen,
I hope you enjoy the
recipes! Tony

COOKING
A BASIC REPERTOIRE
A GUIDE TO EXPLORING FOOD AND COOKING

PRESENTED BY
TONY POLOMBO

iUniverse, Inc.
New York   Lincoln   Shanghai

COOKING
A BASIC REPERTOIRE

iUniverse books may be ordered through booksellers or by contacting:

iUniverse
2021 Pine Lake Road, Suite 100
Lincoln, NE 68512
www.iuniverse.com
1-800-Authors (1-800-288-4677)

ISBN-13: 978-0-595-37866-1 (pbk)
ISBN-13: 978-0-595-82238-6 (ebk)
ISBN-10: 0-595-37866-8 (pbk)
ISBN-10: 0-595-82238-X (ebk)

Printed in the United States of America

In my twenty-five years of teaching I have tried to make people realize that cooking is primarily fun and that the more they know about what they are doing, the more fun it is.

—James Beard, from *Theory and Practice of Good Cooking*

Table of Contents

COOKING
A BASIC REPERTOIRE

Recipe Table of Contents

ENTREES

through. To help keep the chicken moist and flavorful, I provide a recipe for a Greek style marinade that is also excellent on grilled pork or lamb.

Roast Prime Rib of Beef au Jus   58

Still another tender cut of meat but this time we will use the oven for another dry heat method to roast this cut to juicy perfection. Admittedly, this particular cut is an expensive one that is mostly for special occasions but it is still a great dish to have in the repertoire because few dishes are so effortless that produce such special results. To ensure perfect results every time, it is best to use a digital thermometer placed outside the oven which has a cable connection to a probe that is placed inside the meat. Once the meat reaches a selected internal temperature, an alarm alerts the cook to remove the roast.

Sautéed Pork Medallions in a Pan Sauce   63

Cooking tender cut of meats like this on the stovetop gives us a chance to finish it with a pan sauce. What's the big deal about a pan sauce? A pan sauce is the quickest way for the home cook to create something that tastes so good, it is something that one would only expect to find at a fine restaurant. Once you taste it, you will be amazed at what you created which hopefully, will whet your appetite to learn more and keep amazing yourself! (Not to mention your family and friends who will get to taste your creations.)

Breaded Cutlets   68

Another popular way to cook a tender cut of meat on the stove top that gives us great results is to bread it and panfry it. While it is certainly not a difficult dish to make, the steps of breading are a bit more involved and messy than most of the above dishes. But breaded fried food is so good whether it's this dish, chicken cutlets or perhaps breaded pork chops, breaded fish, breaded veal cutlets, and many more. This makes it worthwhile for all cooks to have 'the standard breading procedure' as part of their cooking arsenal.

Barbecued Spare Ribs   72

Spare ribs are a tough but flavorful part of the pig. Here, we are using a low dry heat method, barbecuing which not only tenderizes the meat but also adds additional flavor with smoke. I have adapted a barbecue smoker recipe for use on a covered gas or charcoal grill. If you get hooked and then decide you want to barbecue a lot, you can then buy a smoker that will turn out great results effortlessly.

Sole Amandine   81

This sautéed fish dish with slivered almonds, lemon juice, and finished with a simple butter sauce is delicious. Although it is very easy dish to make, it had been mostly a restaurant dish because of the difficulty in finding fresh sole except at fish markets. Now that many supermarkets are doing a better job of stocking fresh fish, this should be a part of the home cook's repertoire for those households that enjoy fish.

The difference between good and not so good crab cakes is simple. Good crab cakes have lots of crab meat and little breading. Some know how in picking out the right crab meat along with a good recipe that keeps the breading to the minimum amount to keep the crab cake from falling apart is all that's needed for the home cook to effortlessly produce some first rate crab cakes.

Although some people enjoy this as a main dish, it is so rich that others prefer it as a side dish so this is a lead in to the side dishes below. Like many Italian dishes, the secret is simply insisting on the best quality ingredients like genuine Parmigiano-Reggiano cheese to go with the heavy cream and unsalted butter. This is one of the all time great comfort foods!

SIDES

Plain steamed rice with a little butter makes an OK side dish. Rice pilaf takes only a little more effort but is a quantum leap in taste. And if you know how to make rice pilaf, it is only a small step away from learning to make more exotic dishes like risotto, that wonderfully creamy Northern Italian rice dish.

Wouldn't it be nice if we could make a great baked potato as quick as we can grill a steak? This recipe uses a combination cooking method that takes advantage of the microwave's speed and the outdoor grill's concentrated heat to crisp up the skin.

This is one of the easiest and tastiest potato recipes there is. The slightly sweet flavor of these tiny red potatoes adds to the interest.

These have become a standard on many restaurant menus because of their slightly chewy texture which is a change from the standard issue mashed potatoes that don't require any teeth at all to eat!

COOKING
A BASIC REPERTOIRE

My children didn't really like vegetables any more than most other children. But after I made this tasty dish for them the first time, they have regularly requested either this or sautéed spinach made the same way.

This rich side dish is probably best known as a mainstay on steakhouse menus. This version of the classic uses a roux (flour and butter cooked together) thickened milk sauce known as a béchamel sauce as its foundation. Béchamel sauce is the foundation of many popular dishes like macaroni and cheese and that yummy sawmill gravy served on chicken fried steak. I think you will find the section on elementary sauce making to be an especially instructive part of your cooking education.

The difference between a sauce and a cream soup is sometimes little more little more than adding either chicken broth as in this soup or perhaps clam broth if you are making a clam chowder and finishing with a milk product. The dried mushrooms supercharge the mushroom flavor when they are soaked in warm water and added to the soup.

Here is a special salad often associated with fancy restaurants but you will learn to effortlessly make this special treat in your own home in addition to learning everything you ever wanted to know about olive oil to help you in your shopping for this often misunderstood ingredient. And for those of you who want to go the extra mile and make your own croutons instead of using the pre-made ones in a box, I'll show you how. However, these croutons taste so good, you might want to eat them all before you have a chance to put them in the salad. Don't say I didn't warn you!

Acknowledgements

After looking at some of the Acknowledgements sections of some of the other books in my personal library, it really drove home the point that conventional publishing and self-publishing are really worlds apart.

While the conventionally published author often has an assembled army of helpers in place to thank such as the publisher, agent, copy editor, photographer and many more, the self-published author often has to take on these jobs alone to try and keep the expense of producing the book within a modest budget.

But does that mean that the self-published author like me has nobody to thank? Nothing can be further from the truth. Although many of the above mentioned jobs in a self-published book are done by the author, some professional help is needed to have a fighting chance to provide a book that will meet the standards of the bookselling industry. But more importantly, unlike a conventionally published book where an author knows that his book has some value to the world because somebody was willing to pay to publish it, the self-published author has no built-in assurances that anyone will like their book enough to spend their hard earned money to buy it. Without any assurances up front of any success, the self-published author who goes into all of this seeking some commercial success has to first have support and encouragement from those who believe in him. Let's face it, the obstacles to publishing success are formidable and few people are able to see themselves as succeeding unless they are surrounded by people who really show their support. So while the people I thank here may have different roles from the ones being thanked by the conventionally published author, I am no less grateful for their contributions.

Because I did not have the 'platform' of credentials of being previously published or even being a chef, I felt that trying to persuade a conventional publisher to go with me was a long shot and that self-publishing was the way to go. I saw that iUniverse offered me some of the professional support such as editorial reviewing and cover design to give this first all-important effort at publishing the best chance to succeed. As I write this, I have no idea of what will become of this book commercially but Rachel Krupicka who has been my contact at iUniverse during the production of this book has done a wonderful job in patiently and knowledgeably dealing with all of my correspondence for which she deserves a special word of thanks.

Writing a cookbook can also require obtaining permissions from a number of different sources for adapting or reprinting recipes. Rachel referred me to FreelancePermissions.com where Natalie Giboney has been tremendously helpful in dealing with the different publishers on my behalf. And I would be remiss in not thanking all of you who were kind enough to grant me permission to use some of your ideas as part of the foundation of this book. It is my sincere wish that this book will attract many new people into food and cooking who will then become your readers too!

My mother taught me at an early age to appreciate good food by her tireless preparation of daily meals for me and my father. I have tried to pass the torch by introducing good food and cooking to my sons AJ and Chris starting at an early age. I greatly appreciate their support, especially from Chris who lent his artistic talents to the steer and pig drawings in the sections on meat.

And while I'm thanking all of the 'little people', one deserves a special mention. Linda Coyne has been not only a close friend but an endless source of encourage-ment and support. While any good writer will have pride in what he or she has written, there is always that need to have someone to read those words as they emerge to provide feedback and validate their worth. Linda has spent countless hours reading those words not to mention sampling my food. As they say, it's a tough job but somebody's got to do it!

And for those who have spent their hard earned money and/or time to read my book, many of you are friends (too many to mention here) who have lent your words of support for which I offer my heartfelt thanks. But the rest of you don't know me at all since this is my first published work. For you, thanks for taking a chance on me and my work. I hope in turn you will be rewarded with a lifetime of good food and great times in sharing it with others.

Introduction

When it comes to food, most people fall into one of two categories—those who eat to live and those who live to eat.

In one way, I admire those who eat to live. For one thing, these are usually people who don't have a weight problem. On the other hand, I notice that these same people tend to look at food as a commodity. It's pretty much all the same. It would seem unlikely that eat to live types would be interested in cookbooks. Why put the additional effort into cooking from scratch when the taste of convenience foods is perfectly acceptable?

And then there is group I belong to, the live to eat group. Food is not just a way to stay alive but a source of enjoyment in life to be savored. Whatever the food or drink, it is a pleasure to try and find new and better ones to add more enjoyment to our lives. One way to do this is to eat out in a good restaurant as often as we can. However, many of us just can't afford to do this on a regular basis. Affordability aside, there is a great deal of personal satisfaction in being able to cook the foods that I love so much instead of having to rely on others. And then there is the tremendous satisfaction of sharing good cooking with friends and family. All of this drove me to want to learn as much as possible about food and cooking. Although my profession as an engineer kept me from making a full time job of this passion, I did study countless cookbooks obtained from bookstores and libraries and attended evening culinary classes at the local community college to learn about how the professionals practice their craft.

The result is that if I want to, I can prepare a satisfying meal for myself or my family or for others at a social occasion. This is not to say that I don't enjoy eating out from time to time and letting others do the cooking and cleaning. It's just nice to have the choice!

People I talk to during social occasions say that they wish they could cook too. Although cooking is hardly rocket science, my overview of the many cookbooks out there is that there are many recipes but precious little "know how" and explanation of underlying knowledge, especially for the less experienced cook.

Professional cookbooks address this need but can be overwhelming since much of their subject matter is beyond the scope of the home cook.

My aim in creating this cookbook is to not only supply recipes, but also to use many of these recipes as a mini-lesson for providing an understanding of the underlying cooking principles and ingredients. The recipes were selected based on their instructive value along with ease of preparation without the need for expensive kitchen equipment. The intended result is that the reader will not only know how to make a particular dish but also be able to knowledgeably experiment with different variations and perhaps create an even better tasting dish!

When it comes to experimenting with recipes there are different styles ranging from those who follow a recipe religiously to those who feel that a recipe is little more than a rough guideline and an invitation to 'free wheel' it. I'm sure that pop psychologists would diagnose this as left-brained vs. right-brained ways of thinking.

Without trying to put a value judgment on the whole thing, let me offer my thoughts on the subject. I look at a great recipe as being not only a way to create a dish that I really like but more importantly a reliable way to recreate it just the way I want it, time after time. But how do you obtain that great recipe? All you can do is try different recipes and experiment until you finally develop that one that you want as a keeper.

But the road to that great recipe can be a never ending path unless you abide by the following advice:

When you try a new recipe for the first time, try to follow it as exactly as possible, keeping substitutions and improvising to an absolute minimum.

Why? Because it's the only reliable way to know whether you have a good recipe. Put another way, if you follow the recipe carefully and it still doesn't taste the way you like it, you'll know it's the recipe and not the cook. Depending on how far off the mark you are, you can then either decide to make changes in the recipe next time you cook or just go to a new recipe and try again.

Because this book deals with established classic dishes instead of brand new ones, the results are by necessity refinements of existing recipes. Many times I laid 4 or 5 recipes for the same dish side by side, comparing and combining ideas and ingredient combinations. Sometimes this resulting composite recipe is an improvement on all of the others. Sometimes it just results in indigestion. But that's what experimenting is all about!

The recipes in this book are a result of my researching and experimenting, trying to find that great recipe that is a keeper. I hope you find many if not all of these to be keepers. At the very least, I hope to give the reader a good head start on finding that great recipe.

Enjoy the journey!

It's the Ingredients, Stupid!

Sorry about that! I don't want to insult you; I just want to get your attention to make a point.

If you have read this far, you then must appreciate that there is a difference between good food and not so good food—or more exactly, the difference between a good and not so good rendition of a particular dish.

It stands to reason that if you are making something and want the best possible results, you need to have both the best ingredients and the best technique in preparation. But while preparation is important, if the ingredients you are starting out with are substandard, you have already severely limited how good your ultimate result can be no matter how good your preparation is. On the other hand, with first rate ingredients, less than first rate technique will usually lead to a decent result, even if it is not the best it can be.

Insisting on the best ingredients isn't always easy. There are always alternatives out there that cost less but you usually get what you pay for. For example, why do the best crab cakes at good seafood restaurants taste better than the ones that are made mostly of bread? Of course, the answer is that the best crab cakes have the most crabmeat which is expensive. When cooking professionally, realizing an adequate profit is vital and reduction of food costs can often lead to compromises in the ingredient selection process. But when cooking for yourself or those you care for, why compromise?

The other factor is that sometimes the best ingredients for a particular recipe can only be found in a specialty store instead of the supermarket where most of us shop for our everyday food. This is especially true for ethnic foods. The situation is improving as many supermarkets are constantly adding more specialty foods to accommodate their customers.

Having said the above, home cooks have long been frustrated by recipes that get carried away with exotic ingredients. Because these recipes are mainstream classics, the ingredients should not prove to be overly difficult to find, especially for those who live in or near a large city. Unfortunately, those who live in rural areas are going to have more difficulties since sparsely populated areas cannot normally support specialty stores. The only ways around this are to either make periodic trips into the city and stock up or consider ordering by mail or via the Internet since many specialty stores now have a website for the convenience of their customers.

The bottom line is…if you are serious about your food and want each dish you prepare to be as good as it can be, you must be fussy about the ingredients you use. In case you forget this, please refer to the friendly reminder at the beginning of this section.

Some Words About Technique

On the subject of technique, I just wanted to mention what I feel to be the two most common errors of the amateur cook—under seasoning along with the habit of overcooking many foods.

Adequate amounts of salt and pepper, herbs and spices, along with other flavorings like onions and garlic are often vital to make sure that the finished dish isn't bland and unappetizing. This doesn't mean that a dish has to necessarily be spicy hot to be interesting—it just means that it should have enough lively flavors to stimulate the taste buds. Good cooking is more than just presenting a bland dish with salt and pepper on the side for the diner to add and hopefully make the dish palatable. Many times adding seasonings at the beginning of cooking produces better results than just adding them at the end.

To try and prove this to yourself, you can do a simple experiment. Cook up two small separate batches of scrambled eggs in some neutral vegetable oil. For one, mix the amount of salt and pepper you would normally use into the raw eggs. For the other, leave all seasoning out until the cooked product is ready to eat. For most people, the salt and pepper will become an integral part of the flavor profile of the dish when it is mixed into the raw eggs. The other dish will have the taste of the bland eggs with the sharp flavor of the salt and pepper sprinkled on the outside as competition.

It used to be the general opinion in the culinary world that whether meat was salted before or after cooking was not important. But after enough people tasted the results side by side, it is now considered pretty much a fact that adding salt before cooking meat produces better tasting food. This concept has been expanded by some to using a method called *brining* which involves placing food like a whole turkey in a salt water solution before roasting until salt (along with water for moisture) is actually absorbed into the meat fibers to season them.

But there has to be some care taken when using salt. Some people may be on sodium restricted diets. In addition, cooking can involve evaporating some of the water out of a sauce or soup. This can make the food too salty at the end if too much salt was there to begin with. This is why when using canned broths, reduced sodium versions are always recommended.

Even when using the same recipe, a dish may taste a little different each time you cook it. Good cooks taste a dish a number of times during the course of its preparation to see how it is coming along. But tasting at the end before serving is the most important. Recipes may instruct the cook to "correct the seasonings". Sometimes, the seasonings that were added at the beginning of cooking have lost some of their punch from the cooking process. Adding a pinch of those same seasonings at the end will bring them back to life. Sometimes a little salt or pepper or lemon juice is needed to make the finished dish taste the way it's supposed to. That's the cook's job!

Finally, there is the judgment call the cook has to make as to how much salt and other seasonings are appropriate for the people he or she is serving. From my experience, I know that I like a little more salt and a little more spiciness than most other people so I back off a little and invite others to add a touch of extra salt or other seasonings in their own dishes if they wish but this is usually not necessary.

In one regard, overcooking is most understandable since many of those overcooked foods can pose some health risks if they are undercooked. Chicken and pork come to mind. To make sure that these foods are not undercooked, they are often cooked into submission just to make doubly sure that they are absolutely, positively, safe to eat. And safe they are, although there are usually other words to describe the end result—dry, tough, and tasteless come to mind.

It is simply a fact that most foods have an ideal point where the cooking has developed the maximum combination of tenderness, flavor and juiciness. Cooking the food beyond this point does little more than dry it out. (There are some exceptions, like slow cooking in liquid and barbecuing that can tenderize tough meat by long cooking. Even though the juices are squeezed out by this long cooking, tough pieces of meat have lots of connective tissue that is mostly turned into gelatin which makes the meat moist and tender.)

So it comes down to a battle of conflicting priorities. We want our food to be cooked enough so it is safe to eat but we also want it to be as tasty and juicy as possible. The only way to try and balance these desirable priorities is to change ones attitude from "cooking things extra just to make sure" to "cooking things just enough to get by".

This may well mean asking your family member or guest to cut into their food to make sure it is cooked enough for their taste. And although modern conveniences like instant read thermometers eliminate a lot of the guesswork, once in a while you are going to guess wrong and undercook something. Big Deal! So you just cook it a little more and have them try it again. Steak restaurants do it all the time. It is safe to say that most steaks that are sent back to the kitchen are done so because they are undercooked for the diner's taste since undercooked food is a much easier problem to fix than overcooked food.

How Much Cooking Is Enough?

Now that I have raised the issue about food safety and the importance of not overcooking food to make it taste best, it's only fair to explain these sometimes conflicting priorities.

The two main foods we are concerned with from a safety standpoint are meats and eggs. (While under or overcooking vegetables may be undesirable, there is no safety issue involved with them.)

Meats

The only truly reliable way to determine the doneness of meat and poultry other than cutting it and looking at the inside is by measuring the internal temperature with an instant read thermometer. As a practical matter, it is difficult to use a thermometer on a thin piece of meat. But the benefit of it being thin is that after browning it on both sides, the inside should likely be cooked. For thicker cuts of meat, roasts, poultry, etc. an instant read meat thermometer should always be used to determine doneness. Many recipes still give cooking times only but these are guesses that are usually on the conservative side to make sure that the meat is not undercooked. While it's OK to give cooking times as guidelines, for other than thin cuts of meat where a thermometer is not practical I urge you to think of internal temperatures as your target and not cooking times.

But there is a small complication to work around. And that is what is called "carryover" cooking—the tendency for meat to continue cooking once it is removed from the heat source. While the prime rib cooked in a 250°F oven has almost no carryover cooking, meat cooked at higher temperatures can have its internal temperature increase by around 5–10°F after it is removed from the heat which for most people just adds a little margin for error against undercooking. The most practical suggestion is to leave the instant read thermometer in the meat or poultry after it is removed from the heat and let it finish cooking for at least another 10 minutes. If the end result is slightly overdone for your taste, you will know for next time to stop the cooking a few degrees earlier—another great reason to own a probe type instant read thermometer as described in the Equipment section. This finishing of the cooking away from the heat source called "resting" by many cookbooks has the additional benefit of allowing the juices to redistribute inside so when you carve a roast for example, the juices will tend to stay in the sliced meat instead of running all over the cutting board. With the above in mind, we can now move on to recommended internal temperatures for different meats.

For years, cookbooks had been advising cooks to cook items like pork and poultry to internal temperatures of 180 to 185 degrees F. in the interest of food safety. The problem was that the resulting pork and white meat of the poultry came out dry and tasteless.

Since then, it has been recognized that the worm that causes trichinosis, the reason we have traditionally cooked **pork** well done, is killed at 137°F. Now, it is an acceptable practice (some do not agree, of course) to cook pork to an internal temperature of as low as 150°F which results in a slightly pink center. Imagine some cookbooks and even some women's magazines now showing color pictures of cooked pork roasts with a slight pink color in the center. Finally, we have the compromise—safe food that is not overcooked into submission!

As for **poultry**, it has now been acknowledged that white meat (for the sake of flavor and juiciness) is best cooked to a lower internal temperature (about 160 degrees F) than dark meat which still needs to be cooked to about 170 degrees F to develop flavor. Indeed, one of tricky problems in the field of cooking is to try and roast a whole bird so that the dark meat is properly cooked without the white meat becoming overcooked at the same time. White meat (chicken and turkey breasts) cooks significantly faster than dark meat and because it is so lean, is very intolerant of overcooking which will dry it out quickly. Dark meat (all other chicken and turkey parts) takes longer to cook and with its extra fat stays moist even if a bit overcooked. So the most foolproof way to cook chicken and turkey is to cook separate parts instead of the whole birds. This way, the white meat can be watched and taken off the heat as soon as it is cooked while waiting for the dark meat to finish cooking through. If you will notice, the instructions in the Grilled Chicken recipe call for the white meat to be removed at 155°F and the dark meat to be removed at 165–170°F—this will take into account about 5°F of carryover cooking.

Veal is the other common meat that has been traditionally cooked to a well done stage. Recognizing that most veal cuts are very lean (and therefore very dry when overcooked), more recent practice is to cook veal similar to the modern practice for cooking pork, leaving perhaps just a trace of light pink in the middle.

Beef and **lamb** have been served anywhere from raw (e.g. steak tartare, carpaccio, kibbe) to well done. See the Roast Prime Rib of Beef au Jus recipe for guidelines on cooking beef which can also be applied to lamb—but special precautions must be noted for ground meats.

With the well publicized tragedy of deaths attributed to *E. coli* bacteria found in undercooked hamburgers at a fast food restaurant a number of years ago, eating rare let alone raw ground meat poses some risk. *E. coli* bacteria can be introduced into meat if there are improper procedures at the slaughterhouse which contaminate the meat with the animal's intestinal contents. *E. coli* has also been traced to unpasteurized apple cider if some of the apples used are picked up off the ground and contaminated with animal droppings. Fortunately, the bacteria are killed rather easily by cooking. Because of this, even steaks cooked rare are considered to be safe from *E. coli* to eat since any of these bacteria that may be on the outside of the steak will be killed during cooking. Unfortunately, grinding the meat causes any of the harmful bacteria that may be present to be incorporated throughout the meat so the only way to be sure that any *E. coli* bacteria present has been killed is to cook the hamburger until the juices run clear (about 160°F). As long as the hamburger has enough fat content (about 20% as in ground chuck), cooking to this stage should still result in a palatable burger for many if not most people.

For the lover of rare or medium rare hamburger, a way to try and minimize the risk is to buy whole cuts of beef and grind them at home although this doesn't totally eliminate the risk. But wait, there's more!

Eggs

Quick, what do the following foods have in common?

- Homemade mayonnaise
- Hollandaise and béarnaise sauce
- Spaghetti *carbonara*
- Caesar salad
- Chocolate mousse
- Eggnog

The answer is that the authentic versions of these foods (and some others) require either undercooked or raw eggs to make them. And with the fear of salmonella contamination in raw or undercooked eggs, many of these dishes are now on the endangered species list. Many health departments now either discourage or prohibit restaurants from offering authentic versions of these preparations on their menus. While the chances of running into a contaminated egg are pretty small, quantity preparations that restaurants are often required to do can involve the mixing of possibly dozens of eggs together in a single batch. This increases the odds of contamination.

The commercially prepared versions of these foods you buy in the store are made with pasteurized eggs. Fortunately, pasteurized eggs in the shell are now available to the home cook in some supermarkets under the Davidson's brand name. For more information, see their website www.safeeggs.com

Other than buying pasteurized eggs which is pretty expensive for general use, the only way to completely avoid the danger of salmonella poisoning is making eggs that are fried or poached until the yolk is hard. Scrambled eggs have to be cooked until dry. Ugh!

But good sanitation practices (most notably hand washing) can help reduce the risk of salmonella and other food borne illnesses. These include buying eggs that do not have cracks and are refrigerated constantly. However, the salmonella can be part of the egg when it is laid by the hen so even perfect sanitation practices in the kitchen cannot totally eliminate the risk of salmonella if the egg is not completely cooked. What to do?

Basically, this involves a decision of how much risk is tolerable to enjoy what you want to eat. **However, those who are very young, very old, or those whose immune systems are compromised should not be exposed to any risk of this type since salmonella or any other bacterial poisoning could be life threatening to these individuals.**

Dietetically Incorrect

Just like political correctness, there is an issue that keeps the Food Police on full time alert. That is the issue of enforcing the notion that there are "correct" and "incorrect" foods to eat.

We all know what foods we like to eat. Unfortunately, many of those foods have fat to give them moistness and flavor. Fat is also a flavor carrier for other ingredients in a dish. This means that for a manufacturer to offer a low fat alternative to an existing product that they hope will taste as good as the full fat version, it is often necessary to add more salt and sugar to make up for the missing flavor. In addition, animal fat adds flavor of its own to a dish. This is why butter, bacon and lard along with other fats like chicken fat, goose fat, and others have been part of classic cuisine for centuries—especially in the Western world where we have developed more of a craving for fatty foods. I can't help but be amused at the double standard many of us have that it would be unthinkable to use lard but cooking with bacon or sausage fat is OK. For a shameless example of using sausage fat to flavor a dish, see the jambalaya recipe. At least Food Network's Emeril Lagasse is up front about all of this when he proclaims that "Pork fat rules!" Vegetable oils are more "correct" to eat, but except for virgin olive oils, contribute little or no additional flavor to food.

Next time you look through a cookbook, check out the potato recipes. While the naked potato is certainly in the category of healthy foods, it is just not palatable to most of us without some kind of fat added. And let's face it, most potato recipes are just different methods of adding butter, sour cream, cheese or if it is fried, oil. It's about the same story for vegetable dishes in general. Plain ol' steamed or boiled vegetables are healthy, but who wants to eat them?

Unfortunately, this all amounts to another battle of conflicting priorities. Do we want food that tastes as good as it possibly can or do we want to make compromises in the ingredients for the sake of making our food more "healthy"? Most of us have been making some compromises. For example, many of us use margarine instead of butter even though we all know that butter tastes better. Compromises are OK, but at the very least, we should at least know what the real thing is supposed to taste like!

That is why my priority is to present the best tasting food possible, even if it means using ingredients that are "dietetically incorrect". Once you know what the real thing tastes like, you can then decide how best to enjoy a dish if it is not compatible with your dietary lifestyle. This may mean an occasional splurge on special occasions or experimenting with the ingredients, substituting out some of the bad stuff to see if it still tastes good (or at least acceptable). In addition there are an ever growing number of cookbooks that feature "light and healthy" cooking—but this book is not one of them!

Living With the Food Police

You can't eat that!

I'm sure many of us have heard that. But let's face it; heart disease and cancer (the two leading causes of death) are pretty scary things. If we could only discover the right things to eat (and not eat) that would at least make us feel that we have some control over these twin monsters, we could at least breathe a little easier.

One week, we hear that a particular food is good to eat and then next week, a study comes out saying that it's no good for you and that you should cut down or avoid it altogether. Some of the advice is contradictory. After all, experts disagree. Many of us after a while just throw up our hands and decide to turn a deaf ear to it all. That's a shame because some of the advice can be quite worthwhile and can possibly help us to live a longer and healthier life.

Reality says that many of the foods on the "Do Not Eat" list are ones that we simply love too much to ever give up completely. Fortunately, more of the experts are coming to realize that "any and everything, but in moderation" is more practical advice.

The crucial question is how do you sort out the good stuff from the BS especially if you are a layperson? This layperson advocates a two-pronged approach. First of all, it is important to find an expert on health issues whose judgment you can respect. For most of us, that is our physician. But secondly, it is important to try and develop at least a basic understanding on our own of food and health issues and how they affect our well-being. After all, the decisions concerning our lifestyle choices are ultimately ours. We might as well have them be informed choices.

Equipment

Any time somebody takes up a new endeavor, there is always the question of what and how much equipment has to be bought to enjoy something to its fullest without breaking the bank.

In cooking, along with most other endeavors, there are three main pitfalls one must try to avoid in buying equipment.

1. Buying cheap, inferior goods in the hope of saving a buck.

2. Buying overly expensive goods that have features that only a professional can appreciate.

3. Buying items that have such limited uses that they gather dust.

It is important to note that the recommendations given here are for cooking hobbyists. For those who aspire to be professionals, buying the best one can afford makes more sense. I just don't want to do a disservice to any prospective cooking hobbyist by saying that the $150 frying pan is an absolute necessity to enjoy good cooking.

First of all, few items are absolutely indispensable. For example, you can go to one extreme and buy an expensive restaurant grade stove or at the other extreme, cook by lighting a fire and burning wood or go for one of the many choices in between. They all get the job done but better equipment offers more ease and elegance. How much is that worth to you?

Let's start from the most important and basic stuff and then work our way downward in importance. If one can't have everything, it stands to reason that the most important items should have first priority.

Stove

Virtually every professional cook prefers gas over electric burners. I have cooked with both and agree with the almost universal opinion that gas offers far more control over the cooking temperature, especially in the lower heat ranges. Gas and electric ovens are roughly equal in ability but in either case, models with self-cleaning ovens are more costly but worth it to most who own them.

This is no reason to throw out a perfectly good electric range but just something to keep in mind when that range needs replacing or you are moving into a new kitchen without a stove.

Microwave Oven

OK, they say that a microwave oven does little more than defrost and reheat. Although it should get credit for more uses than that, even those two functions alone make it indispensable as far as I am concerned. Before the microwave came along, it was necessary to take something out of the freezer several hours ahead of time to have it defrosted in time for dinner. Now this is no longer necessary—a great advantage for the two worker household.

Although the microwave is famous for not being able to brown food, it does such a good job of reheating food that it is sometimes difficult to tell that the food is a leftover. If so, why not take advantage of what it does well by creating 'leftovers' on purpose? You can brown a whole big package of hot dogs or smoked sausage on the grill or perhaps some breakfast sausage in a large pan. From there, you can store it in the refrigerator for the short term or the freezer for the long term and when you get hungry, all you have to do is a quick reheating instead of having to take the time to light the grill or fire up the stove to brown your food each time. One of the most interesting finds for me at my local warehouse club store was a large bag of frozen pre-cooked breakfast sausage patties. Just take a patty and microwave it for a minute inside some paper towels and it tastes just like it was cooked fresh—without the bother or the greasy mess in the pan to clean up!

One of my other favorite uses of the microwave oven is for making rice. For example, to make a batch of white rice, I set the oven at full power for 5 minutes followed by half power for 17 minutes. Although the rice doesn't get done any quicker than using conventional cooking, the point is that the cooking process can be automated into an idiot proof procedure that produces perfect results time after time.

The latest designs have power ratings of about 900 to 1,000 watts (smaller ratings are less useful) along with a turntable to produce more even heating of the food.

Pots and Pans

There are only two main decisions to be made in shopping for pots and pans. What kind of metal do we want it to be made of and do we want a non-stick cooking surface.

There are two metals that are far more commonly used for pots and pans than any other—aluminum, and stainless steel. Each has its own significant strengths and weaknesses.

Aluminum is inexpensive and also an excellent conductor of heat. The downside is that aluminum will react to acid foods that contact it like tomatoes and wine. The same is true for **copper**, an even better heat conductor but more expensive than aluminum. When a metal reacts with the food, this can impart an unpleasant taste and color to the food.

Stainless steel avoids the downside of reacting with acid foods but it has its own downside in that it is a relatively poor heat conductor. There are some low-end cookware sets out there that are made of all stainless steel. I started out cooking with a set of all stainless steel pots and pans since that was the normal thing most people bought back then. The problem was when I was simmering sauces or chili, there was always a tendency for the food to stick to parts of the bottom of the pot and burn no matter how careful I was. Later I learned that because of the poor conductivity of stainless steel, hot spots would occur where the electric heating element or the gas flame were in contact with the pot. Changing cookware effectively eliminated this problem.

The most common and cost-effective combination is to use aluminum on the exterior of the pan while using a non-stick surface on the inside where the food is. Everybody has a couple of non-stick pans for cooking eggs, pancakes, and other delicate foods like fish. The popularity of non-stick pans is no mystery; they are easy to clean and there is the health angle in that a non-stick pan requires less fat to cook food. By all means get a couple of inexpensive 9 and 12 inch non-stick pans (T-FAL and Farberware are good and widely available brands among others). It is possible to buy expensive non-stick pans but with heavy use, even the best non-stick surfaces will wear out which will mean that you will still have to replace them. To keep the cooking surface of your non-stick pans in good shape for as long as possible, take care of the pans even to the point of babying them. This means not using any utensils on them except wooden ones or other utensils with a coating designed not to scratch non-stick surfaces. In addition, you are better off hand washing instead of putting non-stick pans in the dishwasher. Dishwashing soap is hard on non-stick surfaces. And finally, do not put the pan on a high heat source for any but a brief period of time—especially when empty. It is believed that extended high heat of a non-stick surface without food has the potential to give off vapors that can be harmful to small creatures like pet birds.

However, non-stick pans are not best for everything. When it comes to browning meat and making pan gravies, a pan with a conventional stainless steel interior cooking surface does the best job. Besides browning the meat better because the interior surface is designed to withstand high heat, the conventional pan accumulates much more of a collection of caramelized pan drippings (*fond*) that stick to the bottom of the pan as a result of cooking the meat. These drippings when dissolved with some liquid (*deglazing*) contribute tremendous flavor to a pan gravy that a non-stick pan cannot match. It is for this reason that non-stick pans have a rather limited acceptance among the world's chefs except for tasks like cooking omelets and fish.

Pans that are both good heat conductors but don't react to acid foods without resorting to an interior non-stick surface require more sophisticated designs which unfortunately translates to a higher price tag. Some manufacturers like All-Clad introduced a sandwich style of bonding layers of stainless steel on the outside around an internal layer of aluminum or copper. These are great pans but quite expensive for the non-professional cook. A less expensive and more common design is to permanently bond a copper or aluminum pad onto the bottom of the stainless steel pan. And Calphalon popularized *anodized aluminum* which has undergone an electrochemical process which keeps it from reacting with acid foods. But a disadvantage of anodized aluminum is that it is not suitable for the dishwasher unlike cookware with a stainless steel surface. In addition, these darker colored pans make it a bit more difficult to determine whether the onions or shallots in the making of a pan sauce are browning or perhaps burning.

So in addition to the non-stick pans, please consider investing in at least a large (11 or 12 inch) sauté pan and a large saucepan (sometimes known as a Dutch oven) with a stainless steel interior/exterior and an aluminum or copper pad built into the base for good heat conductivity. Make sure you have a tight fitting lid for each of these too. For boiling pasta, a large 6 quart stainless steel pot with a lid will do the job inexpensively. There are pots that have pasta inserts that eliminate the need to pour all of the pasta and water into a colander, but they are usually more expensive. Finally, there are occasions where it makes sense to put your pans in the oven or under the broiler to finish the cooking process. This is why pots and pans aimed at the serious cook have bare metal handles instead of the more familiar plastic ones that would melt if placed in an oven or under a broiler.

As mentioned above, plastic or plastic coated utensils and wooden spoons (instead of metal utensils) should be used with non-stick pans to preserve their cooking surfaces from scratching. The same care should be given to good pots and pans with a stainless steel cooking surface because these will also scratch if used with metal utensils.

New brands and models of pots and pans come out pretty often. For recommendations on what brand at what price is best for you, I would suggest finding some knowledgeable salespeople in cookware departments or consult *Consumer Reports* and/or *Cook's Illustrated* magazines; both do testing of cookware and accept no advertising so they can provide independent opinions on products by brand name.

Knives

Once upon a time, all knives were made of **carbon steel**. Because carbon steel is so soft, it can be sharpened easily to a razor-like edge. But because it is so soft, it loses its edge quickly and constantly needs re-sharpening when heavily used. In addition, carbon steel knives will turn dark from oxidation over time because they react to acid foods.

To address the issues of having to re-sharpen the blade and oxidation, the natural progression was to introduce the **stainless steel** knife. Because the metal didn't oxidize and was so hard, an edge lasted much longer before it went dull. This is also why stainless steel razor blades were introduced a number of years ago to take the place of the old conventional carbon steel razor blades. However, even stainless steel razor blades grow dull and have to be replaced. The same is true with stainless steel knives since the metal is so hard it cannot be effectively sharpened. It is even difficult to produce a truly sharp cutting edge on a pure stainless steel knife when it is first made. This is probably why most stainless steel knives sold have serrated edges to try and make them cut well enough to be useful. But a serrated edge makes slicing and dicing vegetables more difficult than with a smooth sharp edge that glides through what it is cutting without grabbing. Serrated edge blades are great bread knives though.

The great compromise emerged in the form of high carbon stainless steel. It doesn't rust and keeps an edge for longer than a carbon blade. And when it eventually gets dull, it can be sharpened (although it is recommended that you take your knives to a cutlery shop to have that done professionally). For these reasons, high carbon stainless steel knives are used almost exclusively by professional and avid amateur cooks (except for a few old fashioned diehards who still insist on a carbon steel knife.) Within the high carbon steel category is a choice of *forged* or *stamped* construction. A forged knife provides better heft and balance that experienced cooks prefer but it requires much more labor to produce and therefore costs more than stamped designs.

The chef's knife is the cooking tool used probably more often than any other. Once a cook gets used to using a fine knife, it almost becomes an extension of his or her hand. Different knives have different weighting and shapes that affect how comfortable each is to use. The only practical advice here is to go to a good cookware or cutlery store that carries high carbon stainless steel knives and get some advice and hopefully an opportunity to hold the knives and judge whether they would be comfortable to you to use for an extended time. Henckel's, Friedr. Dick, and Wustof-Trident are probably the favorite brands among culinary school students and professionals. Other brands which can often be found in various department stores can offer decent quality at attractive prices. Once again, consult *Consumer Reports* and/or *Cook's Illustrated* magazines for the latest brand ratings.

Just remember, if a knife is said to never need sharpening, that's another way of saying that you have a stainless steel knife that *cannot* be sharpened. Any knife will get dull with enough use; the question is whether you can then sharpen the knife or have to throw it away.

Most manufacturers offer many different sizes and types of knives. Once you get past the chef's knife and the small paring knife, you are getting into specialized knives that may be better to buy later if they are really needed unless you get a good deal that includes some extra knives. For the beginning cook, look for a starter set that includes an 8 inch chef's knife, a paring knife, honing steel, and a knife block to hold them all. (Some object to knife blocks because if dirt or grime gets inside the slots where the knives are stored, they are difficult to clean. But this is still better than throwing them in a drawer with other utensils.) In addition, some starter sets may include a serrated bread knife. If the set you are looking at doesn't, a cheap stainless steel knife will do for this purpose. And please don't put your good knives in the dishwasher!

A word about the honing steel, the part of the knife set that looks like a sword…It is not used to actually sharpen the knife but its value is in keeping an already sharp knife edge that way for as long as possible. If the steel is used each time the knife used, the knife will not likely need to be sharpened any more than once every year or two for the average home cook. Once the knife finally does get dull, there are a number of knife sharpeners on the market but most of them are difficult to use or will take off too much of the metal, resulting in a premature end to your knife. As recommended earlier, cutlery stores offer professional sharpening for as little as $3 to $5 per knife. At that price, why mess with anything else?

Cutting Boards

We don't want to cut on a surface that's harder than the knife which is a sure way to quickly dull the knife. The old reliable through the years had been a simple wooden cutting board. However, plastic cutting boards have been growing in favor because of the fear of bacterial contamination remaining in the wooden boards after their use. Unlike the wooden boards, plastic (polyethylene) boards can be placed in the dishwasher and sterilized after each use. Even so, scrubbing a wooden board with warm soap and water has been shown to be adequate in keeping the boards safely clean. To make extra certain, the board can then be wiped down with a diluted solution containing chlorine bleach (about 3 teaspoons per gallon of water).

Hand Tools

By hand tools I mean gadgets that are more specialized cooking aids not routinely found in every kitchen…but should be found in yours!

Dry Measuring Cups—These along with measuring spoons are essential for measuring dry ingredients like flour, salt, sugar, etc. The Pyrex glass measuring cup is only suitable for measuring liquid but is also useful for jobs like heating liquids or melting butter in the microwave. Dry measuring cups and spoons will also do an adequate job of measuring liquid.

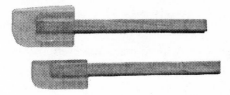

Silicone Spatulas—I use these countless times for cleaning that last bit of food out of a jar, pan or serving dish. They are also nice for stirring food in your sauté pan while cooking as long as you insist on a heat resistant design—and you should!

Instant Read Thermometer—The most common use for this device is to determine whether a piece of meat is cooked to the desired doneness by quickly (about 10–15 seconds) measuring the internal temperature instead of having to cut it with a knife to check the doneness. Most people, who do not use these types of thermometers, use the "cook it into submission just to make sure" method. If you want to convert to the "cook it just enough to get by" method, this device is a must. Taylor and Polder are the most common brands I see in stores although there are other models out there that look to be identical units except for the brand name. The LCD digital version is much easier to read and use than an analog model with a dial and needle. If 10–15 seconds is too long to wait for a temperature reading and you can afford the $85 price tag, the ThermoWorks Thermapen which can provide readings in as little as 4 seconds is available from www.thermoworks.com

The instant read thermometer is different from the old oven meat thermometers with thick stems that were left in the meat throughout their cooking time. To use an instant read thermometer, the pointed tip is inserted into the meat (avoiding fat or bone which would result in false readings) for about 10–15 seconds until the final temperature is registered and then is removed since the dial on an instant read thermometer display cannot withstand oven temperatures. But repeatedly opening the oven door to check the temperature of the roast loses heat and time to get the oven back up to temperature.

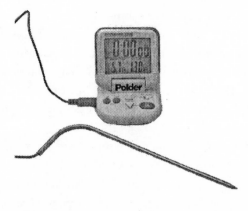

A number of years ago, Polder introduced a thermometer/timer to the marketplace (other brands are now available) that has the instant read digital temperature display unit safely outside of the oven but connected by a long wire to a probe which can be inserted into the meat and left there during its cooking time. The wire is slender and flexible enough that the oven door can be shut over it without harm. The unit can be programmed to give off an audible signal when a pre-selected internal temperature of the meat is reached. No more overcooked roasts!! Every kitchen should have at least the instant read if not both of these types of thermometers.

Whisk—Many of us first saw a wire whisk as a tool for TV chefs to make meringue by hand in a copper bowl. Metal wire whisks are more efficient for heavy duty chores like mixing thick liquids or batters. But a 10 or 11 inch nylon whisk like the one pictured will enable you to efficiently and thoroughly hand mix most ingredients together and bring them to a smooth consistency without the worry of scratching your cookware like with a metal wire whisk; perhaps you may want to own one of each. Once you get one of these, you will be surprised how often you use it.

Spring Loaded Tongs—Just like a fine knife, a good set of tongs will become an extension of your hand for turning meat over a grill or over a hot pan in addition to handling hot ears of corn. Look for a relatively large pair (about 11" long) which will keep your hands away from the intense heat of a hot grill. The scissors type tongs are not quite as good since they have the tendency to crush the food. In addition, they are hard on the finger joints, especially those that may be stiffening up from arthritis.

Lemon Reamer—For most dishes that use lemon juice, freshly squeezed lemon juice is superior to the bottled stuff. A wooden lemon reamer is the most efficient tool to extract the juice if small quantities are needed. The juice can be passed through a strainer to remove the seeds.

Garlic Press—There are some food experts who do not believe in using a garlic press, preferring to chop all garlic with a knife. They feel that using the garlic press releases the aromatic oils too quickly although it is unclear whether this really affects the end result. When I need minced garlic in a hurry, I let the garlic press do the work. The Zyliss Susi model shown is the one I and many other cooks have depended on for some time now.

Vegetable Peeler—Of course it peels potatoes, apples and the like. It also does more elegant things like cheese shavings for your Caesar salad and chocolate shavings for your desserts. The Oxo model shown here is quite popular because of the comfortable non-slip handle common to all of their products along with the sharp peeling edges that make quick work out of a sometimes not so pleasant chore.

Meat Pounder—The style I prefer has a heavy metal round disk with a handle attached to the middle. It does a better job than the old hammer style pounders that can have a tendency of ripping holes in the meat. But since this is harder to find than the hammer style, the latter will do if that is the only available choice. The model in the picture is from Italy but Oxo now offers a round disk model. This is admittedly a specialized tool but if you have the need for converting a boneless chicken breast into a flat, delicate replica of veal scaloppini, it is worth having.

Box Style Cheese Grater—This is an old fashioned device that as far as I am concerned, has never been adequately replaced—. but the Microplane grater sure comes close! The food processor does the job of grating cheese with far less effort, but the finished cheese has more of a consistency of sawdust rather than the very fine strands of cheese that come out of a hand held grater. The course slots shown do a nice job of shredding soft cheeses so you don't have to spend the extra money for pre-shredded cheese. By the way, the very fine teeth on the side of the grater do a passable job of grating whole nutmeg so you won't need to buy a nutmeg grater unless you use freshly ground nutmeg quite often. Look for a non-stick model to avoid the problem of grated cheese sticking to the grating surface.

Microplane Zester/Grater—This tool looks like something from a woodworking shop from which it was adapted for kitchen use. It doesn't grate cheese quite as finely as the box style grater but the sharp cutting surfaces make quick work out of grating hard cheeses. For recipes that call for grated zest (the colorful outside flesh of citrus fruits containing flavorful oils) this tool does it best. And it is super for grating nutmeg. This hand tool has become an instant classic and a must have for the serious cook.

Food Mill—This is another old fashioned tool that was a standard part of our grandmother's kitchen for pureeing fruits and vegetables into applesauce, baby foods, and the like but is a rarity in today's kitchen with access to already processed foods from the supermarket. Nothing duplicates the food mill's ability to puree a tomato, passing the pulp through while at the same time, straining out the skins and seeds. Heavy duty stainless steel models can cost over $100 but plastic models like the Moulinex shown in the picture do an adequate job for the home cook for about $20–25. Look for a model with 3 interchangeable metal disks with different sized holes. The one with the medium sized holes is probably best for making tomato sauce. The large holes are good for making homemade applesauce and you don't even have to peel the apples first!

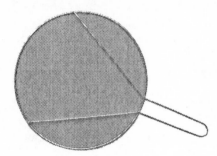

Splatter Screen—This inexpensive gadget allows you to sauté food without a lid so it browns instead of steaming but also helps to keep the splattering grease from making a mess out of the stove. This is also especially useful when simmering a tomato sauce.

Pepper Mill—Black peppercorns that you grind yourself taste far superior to pre-ground pepper. Lose the pre-ground pepper. Be sure that the mill you buy has adjustments for obtaining either a fine or course grind.

Salad Spinner—This is admittedly a gimmicky looking device. But salad lovers know that absolutely dry greens are important to avoid watering down the salad dressing. Lots of paper towels will also do the job but when you are tired of wasting all of those paper towels, you will consider buying a salad spinner. This Oxo model shown here is considered to be one of the very best available.

Electric Tools

Recommending various hand tools is easier than recommending electric tools. Because the various electric tools can be quite expensive, the amount of money wasted as the result of a not so good recommendation can be substantial. You will find that most experienced cooks have all of these items in their kitchen. But are they an appropriate purchase for the novice cook? That is a tough call. Some of these items may do little more than gather dust about 99% of the time, but that one occasional time you really need it, it may be a life saver. Does that make that item worth having as a part of your kitchen? Only you can answer that.

Presented in the order of increasing price we have…..

Immersion Blenders—While the food blender has been around for several decades, the immersion blender (sometimes called a stick or hand blender) has been around for considerably less time. Its main claim to fame is the ability to do its thing within a pot of cooking food without the need to pour all of the liquid into a conventional food blender and back again. In addition, the used blender requires a cleanup job while the immersion blender can simply be rinsed off under running water.

I bought one on a lark but found that it was a rather handy device. For example, if a tomato sauce still has too many vegetable pieces after cooking and I want a smoother consistency—no problem. A quick hit with the immersion blender will give me that smoother consistency in a hurry.

The other skill that these machines excel in is making emulsified sauces like mayonnaise. (Emulsifying is getting two normally unmixable liquids to combine together in suspension.) The instruction leaflet that came with the immersion blender I bought included a recipe for mayonnaise that called for cracking an egg into a glass measuring cup and pouring about a cup of vegetable oil over the top of it. After holding the running blender in place at the bottom of the cup for a few seconds, a mysterious white substance emerged from the bottom of the oil. Then a few seconds later, the white substance swallowed up all of the oil. The brute force of the immersion blender in a confined space instantly whipped up some freshly made mayonnaise. Neat stuff!

Some models like the Braun shown in the picture even have a mini-chopper attachment which attaches on the end of the unit which will chop small amounts of onions, garlic, nuts and the like.

Blenders—OK so if an immersion blender is so great, what do you use a conventional full sized blender for? The short answer is drinks like milk shakes, smoothies and frozen daiquiris along with soups that have to be pureed to a totally smooth consistency, something that immersion blenders and food processors cannot quite do. While working on a Cream of Vegetable Soup recipe, I found that using an immersion blender did a so-so job but when I totally liquefied the vegetables in the blender, the vegetable taste (and color) finally permeated the soup and I knew that using a blender was the only way to do this dish properly.

Food Processors—When the food processor first came out, it was hailed as perhaps the greatest labor saving device ever to come to the kitchen. But like the other devices, it has its strengths and weaknesses. Its strength is the ability to puree solid foods that a blender has a difficult time handling. For example, it is hard to imagine making hummus (pureed chick pea dip) with anything else but a food processor. But the food processor has a more difficult time with very liquidy foods which can leak out of the processing bowl. Blenders handle these better.

Food processors are also good at blending solid ingredients together for making pasta and bread dough along with pie crusts for those who don't want to do these rather strenuous jobs by hand.

Using the various disk attachments, food processors can slice fruits and vegetables and make large amounts of fries or coleslaw in lightning fast time. Perhaps the most common use of the food processor is to use the metal blade to finely chop vegetables. Although this saves a lot of labor, many chefs prefer the old fashioned hand cutting of vegetables with a knife instead of the food processor which tends to turn vegetables like onions into a slushy mess, especially if finely chopped vegetables are desired.

Large Cuisinart and to a lesser extent KitchenAid food processors are a mainstay of the experienced cook who prepares a large number of different foods from scratch. But they are too expensive ($200 and up) and likely to gather dust in the inexperienced cook's kitchen. On the other hand a mini-chopper which will do small amounts of onions, garlic, nuts and the like run about $40 and are popular with those who don't want to do their chopping with a knife.

Stand Mixers—These have a variety of uses from making mashed potatoes to whipping cream and beating egg whites into a meringue. Then there are the more heavy duty jobs like mixing dough for bread. Cooks who usually stick with the light duty jobs like mashing potatoes will normally use the commonly available and reasonably priced Sunbeam stand mixers (or even an electric hand mixer). Those who are into the heavy duty jobs that require more motor horsepower, or those who just like serious power tools and attachments will spring the bucks (about $175 and up) for a KitchenAid mixer shown in the picture.

In summary, each of these small electric appliances do some things better than all of the others which is why most experienced cooks have all of these items in their kitchens. But the less experienced cook at least when starting out has a much smaller repertoire of dishes and should carefully consider which of these would be useful enough to justify the money spent on them. I would suggest starting out with a conventional full size blender and perhaps a hand mixer (although a hand held whisk may well be enough) and go from there as your experience and repertoire progresses.

ENTREES

Yes, there is a method to my madness! I have started with the entrees because these are the cornerstone of a basic cooking repertoire. Simple side dishes can fill in nicely until the cook wants to get more ambitious. Desserts can be purchased from bakery departments at your supermarket or if you are lucky enough to still have one in your neighborhood, a bakery shop. Even among chefs, those who concentrate only on desserts, pastry chefs are a breed apart. Baking requires a lot of precision in adhering to formulas to make sure the end result turns out correctly.

To get you started, the first set of dishes are essentially one-pot meals (if you don't count boiling the water for the pasta). These should be simple confidence builders for you.

Unless one is a vegetarian, meat is the centerpiece of most of our meals—especially at dinnertime. Therefore, selecting and cooking meat is a fundamental skill that a cook should learn. The dishes go from beef to chicken to pork with a variety of different representative techniques for cooking them. For those who would like to acquire a more thorough working knowledge of selecting meat, additional material is offered in the Appendix.

Finally, to round out the entrée repertoire, there are some seafood dishes to serve as an introduction to preparing some of the exciting selections available at seafood counters in more and more stores nowadays.

Pasta with Tomato Sauce and Meatballs

When I was growing up, jarred spaghetti sauce was pretty awful. Growing up in an Italian household, there was no other option than sauce made from scratch. As a practical matter, I realize that countless people rely on sauce out of a jar all the time and truth be told, the best of the sauces have come a long way since then. Even so, I firmly believe that a well made sauce from scratch using quality canned tomatoes is better than anything you can buy in a jar. I invite you to try this easy to make sauce for yourself so you can make up your own mind. The only special equipment needed is an inexpensive plastic food mill to puree the tomatoes while leaving the skins and seeds behind.

The meatball recipe is a tasty one and as a bonus, needs only some small modifications to make **a tasty meatloaf recipe**…just delete the grated cheese and add ¼ cup of tomato ketchup and 2 tablespoons of Worcestershire sauce into the meat when mixing. Instead of making the meat into a loaf, sauté them as meatballs or perhaps flatten them out a bit to make them thick patties. It's the browning on the outside that makes all the difference!

Two types of tomato sauces…It may seem simplistic, but of all of the different tomato sauces that exist, there are those made from tomato concentrate (tomato paste and/or puree) and those made from either fresh or canned tomatoes and reduced down to a sauce consistency.

Most of us are familiar with sauces made from tomato concentrate. If you look at the ingredients list of almost all jarred sauces, the first ingredient will be tomato puree (tomato paste, water). There are good reasons for this. For one, this makes the sauce much cheaper to produce than those from whole tomatoes. The other reason is that sauces made from tomato concentrate have more tomato flavor 'punch'. Indeed, I have to admit that the tomato sauces I grew up with and liked were made from puree.

But later in life, I tried marinara sauces made from either fresh tomatoes or canned tomatoes packed in juice and had a wonderful revelation. What these sauces lacked in flavor 'punch' were more than compensated by revealing the beautiful complex flavor profile of a tomato that wasn't over processed.

For those who wish to simplify this dish, simply substitute about ½ pound of bulk Italian sausage or ground beef in place of the meatballs, sauté in a separate pan until brown and then add to the simmering sauce.

This recipe makes enough sauce for about 1 pound of pasta which will serve 3–4 people. The number of meatballs the recipe yields will likely be enough for some tasty leftovers or perhaps to freeze for a future batch of sauce. To prepare the pasta, boil it in at least a gallon of water with a small handful of table salt. Use the pasta manufacturer's times on the back of the box as a guideline but be sure to test the pasta near the end of the cooking time to ensure that it is not overcooked. The cooked pasta should be tender but still have a little bit of chew left in it or as the Italians call it, *al dente.*(to the tooth).

Ingredients	Procedure
• 3 tablespoons extra virgin olive oil • 1 medium onion, chopped finely • 1 teaspoon dried basil • 1 teaspoon red pepper flakes • 1 teaspoon kosher salt • 1 teaspoon freshly ground black pepper	1. Heat the oil in a large saucepan over medium heat. Add the onions and sauté until transparent, stirring occasionally to keep them from burning. 2. Stir in the dried basil, red pepper flakes, salt, and pepper into the onions.
• 2 cloves of garlic, minced • 4 oz. sliced mushrooms, preferably fresh • ½ cup dry white wine	3. Add the garlic and sauté until it gives off an aroma. 4. Stir in the basil and cook for another minute. 5. Add the sliced mushrooms and allow most of their liquid to cook off. 6. Stir in the wine and allow to boil and reduce by about three quarters.

Ingredients	*Procedure*
• 28 oz. can Italian plum tomatoes packed in juice	7. Pass the tomatoes through a food mill into the saucepan. (Alternatively, a blender can be used to puree the tomatoes and seeds but this tends to aerate the tomatoes giving them an odd pink color.) 8. Simmer on low heat uncovered for 60–90 minutes or until the sauce reaches the desired thickness, stirring occasionally. 9. Correct seasonings, adding salt, black pepper, and red pepper flakes to taste.

While the sauce is simmering the meatballs can be prepared...

Meatballs

Ingredients	*Procedure*
• 1 lb. ground beef • 3 cloves of garlic, minced • 1 medium onion, chopped finely • ¾ cup Italian seasoned bread crumbs • ½ cup imported Pecorino Romano cheese, grated (or more to taste)	1. Place the ground beef in the bottom of a mixing bowl large enough to comfortably hold the meatball ingredients while hand mixing. Add the remaining meatball ingredients to the mixing bowl and knead together by hand until thoroughly mixed. Add a little water if the mixture seems too dry.

Ingredients	*Procedure*
• 2 teaspoons dried basil • 4–5 tablespoons fresh Italian flat leaf parsley, chopped finely • 1 egg • 2 teaspoons kosher salt • 2 teaspoons freshly ground black pepper	
• Olive or vegetable oil for pan frying	2. Using your hands and wetting them regularly, form the mixture into balls about 1½ inches in diameter and place in a large sauté pan with enough oil to cover the bottom of the pan. Brown on all sides using medium heat turning frequently. (Alternatively, the meatballs can be baked in a 375 degree oven until brown, about 30 to 40 minutes.) 3. Place the browned meatballs into the simmering sauce mixture for its last 30 minutes or so of cooking time. Before serving, degrease the surface of the sauce if necessary.

A few more words...

Not all tomatoes are alike... The plum tomato with more flesh and less liquid is more suitable for making fine sauce than other varieties that may be better for eating out of hand. Vine ripened tomatoes unquestionably taste better than tomatoes that are picked green (because of their durability) and then allowed to ripen or gassed with ethylene to speed up the process.

The only time and place one can buy top notch vine ripened tomatoes is at harvest time at a farmer's market. This is nice during the month or two during the peak tomato season. But during the other months of the year, an excellent canned tomato which is picked at the peak of ripeness is a more consistent product which is why the recipe is standardized on canned tomatoes.

Among canned tomato connoisseurs, the San Marzano tomato, a plum variety grown in the volcanic soil near Naples, Italy is the gold standard. They are indeed excellent. If you can find these (usually at an Italian grocery store) for a reasonable price, buy them. But there are also other very good canned plum tomatoes packed in juice from both Italy and the United States. Let price, availability, and your palate be your guide. Also note I mentioned 'packed in juice'. Make a point of looking for tomatoes packed in juice instead of puree to get that fresh tomato taste you are looking for in the first place. Having said this, it should be pointed out that the labeling on the tomatoes packed in Italy can be somewhat inconsistent.

While a marinara sauce is very light in body and cooked only minimally, for me the standard tomato sauce for pasta has to have a bit more flavor intensity and body to be able to coat the pasta adequately. To do this I simmer the sauce for about 60–90 minutes to cook out some of the water. This intensifies the flavors but still preserves the tomato character which wouldn't happen if adding tomato paste to try and accomplish the same thing.

The two main cheeses that are used with pasta are *pecorino* and *Parmesan* cheeses. If you will take the time to learn about and buy authentic versions of these products, the quality of your finished product will be way ahead of the many that resort to bogus shortcuts to save time.

Authentic *pecorino* is a sheep's milk cheese made in different regions of Italy. The kind most available by far in the U.S. is associated with Rome and is therefore called Pecorino Romano. Many use the terms 'pecorino' and 'Pecorino Romano' interchangeably because of this although this is not quite correct. There are even brands of Pecorino Romano sold like Locatelli. Mostly all versions of pecorino are pungent and salty. This doesn't translate well to eating out of hand but it makes for an assertive condiment to spicy tomato sauces where the milder Parmesan would get lost. As long as you buy pecorino imported from Italy and grate it yourself, you are likely to get a quality product.

Parmesan is the generic name given by many people for grating cheese that is sprinkled on something with tomato sauce. The gold standard for this type of cheese is *Parmigiano-Reggiano*, a wonderfully complex, nutty tasting cheese that comes from Emilia-Romagna, a region in northern Italy that includes Bologna and Parma that is especially famous for its food products. It is considered by most cheese aficionados as being one of the world's great cheeses and is often eaten out of hand. However, because this cheese is so expensive due to the time consuming manufacturing and aging involved, there are many imitators from both Italy and around the world offered as alternatives. For my money, if I am making a fettuccine Alfredo or a Caesar salad, nothing tastes as good as the original. But it's your money and if you need to use a substitute Parmesan cheese because of price or availability, at least buy it by the piece and grate it yourself. The taste of the pre-grated stuff in the cardboard can is definitely inferior to the real thing.

The meatballs are sautéed in olive oil because it has more flavor than vegetable oil but either is OK. Extra virgin olive oil is not necessary for sautéing and has a tendency to burn although some people add a little of it to the sauce for flavoring just before serving.

The most popular method of browning the meatballs is to sauté them in a frying pan which produces a fine flavor and a pleasing dark crust. However, baking them produces a result that is almost the same without requiring the meatballs to be turned while cooking. Although the meatballs in this recipe are made of beef, some cooks add ground pork and/or veal to the mixture just like meatloaf is often made.

The bread crumbs used here are dried (either seasoned or plain). If fresh bread crumbs are used, more are needed. In general, more bread crumbs in the mixture produces a more tender meatball but too much can make the meatballs mushy.

In general, it should be noted that the proportions of the meatball ingredients are very much subject to personal taste. It is suggested to use this recipe as a guideline and before cooking, make a small patty out of the meat mixture and sauté it in a frying pan. Your taste will tell you what adjustments (if any) you need to make.

Chili con Carne

This is a Tex-Mex classic that is technically a stew. That means that it uses a low moist heat method to tenderize tougher cuts of meat. While the original version likely used cubed beef, a satisfactory and simpler version of this dish can be made with ground meat (or even a combination of cubed and ground meats for a more interesting texture).

There are as many versions of this dish as there are cooks. And almost nobody agrees about which version is the authentic rendition. While I can't settle that issue here, I will say that the version presented here is tasty and easy to prepare. It has tomatoes and some beans (which can be left out if desired). And it has a very thick consistency that you can almost eat with a fork. While some chili cooks like to use beer as their cooking liquid of choice, I like this version that uses a dry red wine. If after making this version, you decide to become a chili connoisseur, you can always experiment with different versions and combinations of ingredients to come up with your own classic.

Other than that, the recipe has a lot of similarities to the tomato meat sauce except that for the tomato meat sauce it was all about the subtlety of complex flavors of the tomatoes while here, we have a collection of robust flavors that will jump out and capture the attention of your taste buds!

Ingredients	*Procedure*
• 3 pounds ground beef,* preferably chuck • 1 tablespoon kosher salt • 1 tablespoon vegetable oil * Or any combination of ground beef, ground pork, or bite-sized cubes of chuck steak.	1. In a large skillet over medium-high heat, sprinkle the salt over the beef and brown it in the vegetable oil. Drain and discard any rendered fat.

Ingredients	Procedure
• 3 tablespoons vegetable oil • 2 garlic cloves, finely chopped • 2 cups celery, finely chopped • 2 cups onions, finely chopped • 2 cups green bell peppers, finely chopped • 1 teaspoon kosher salt • 5 tablespoons chili powder • 1 tablespoon ground cumin	2. In a stockpot, sauté the garlic, celery, onions, green pepper and salt in about 3 tablespoons of vegetable oil over medium-high heat, stirring frequently until translucent—approximately 7–8 minutes. Add the chili powder and cumin to the vegetable mixture and sauté another 2–3 minutes while continuing to stir frequently to keep the spice mixture from burning.
• 1 (28 ounce) can whole tomatoes • 1 (15 ounce) can stewed tomatoes • 1 (6 ounce) can tomato paste • 1 cup dry red wine • 2 whole bay leaves	3. Transfer the browned beef to the stockpot and add the tomatoes (including the juice), tomato paste, red wine, and bay leaves. Cover and bring to a boil and then turn the heat down to medium-low and simmer uncovered for about an hour, stirring occasionally to keep the mixture from sticking to the bottom of the pot. Use the stirring spoon to break up the tomatoes into the desired consistency.

Ingredients	Procedure
• 1 (15 ounce) can kidney beans, drained (optional) • 2 teaspoons cayenne pepper plus additional salt, black pepper, and chili powder (or to taste)	4. Remove the bay leaves and discard. Add the optional kidney beans. Adjust seasonings, cayenne pepper and/or cayenne pepper sauce for more heat as desired. Add additional salt, black pepper, and chili powder to taste. Let stand for at least an hour if possible. (Overnight in the refrigerator is even better.) Skim away and discard any visible fat that may have risen to the surface. Heat and serve. SERVES 6–8.

A few more words...

- Cumin is the one ingredient that is the most responsible for making chili taste like chili and not like a tomato meat sauce for pasta. While chili includes chili powder which consists of ground dried chili peppers and some cumin, most recipes include additional cumin to give this dish its characteristic flavor.

- A technique worth mentioning here is the cooking of the spice mixture (here the chili powder and cumin) in with the cooking fat and vegetable mixture. This heat applied in the presence of fat releases a lot of the flavor essences in the spices and uses the fat as a flavor vehicle to make sure that every spoonful of the dish is perfectly seasoned. This is a recurring theme in Paul Prudhomme's cookbook recipes.

- A variable you can adjust to your taste is the cooking time. The original recipe I adapted this from calls for 2½ hours of cooking. But even after a half hour of cooking and trying a taste, you may find the still firm vegetables and fresh flavors to be appealing enough to stop the cooking right there! I have given an hour of cooking time as a middle of the road guideline. Still more cooking time (but with the cover on) may be required to tenderize any cubed beef you may decide to use. The bottom line is that good cooking is subject to individual preferences. Don't just blindly follow a recipe! Taste your work in progress and make adjustments in the seasoning or cooking times that please you!

• Both *stewing* and *braising* are often used to describe the method of tenderizing tough cuts of meat by cooking them slowly in a covered pot with liquid, usually after browning the meat to add flavor. The differences are pretty subtle. In general, a *stew* consists of cubed meat that is submerged in the cooking liquid. A *braise* normally has whole cuts of meat that are partially submerged in the cooking liquid. With the cover on, the steam produced helps in the cooking. If using all or mostly ground meat in the chili recipe, covering is not required because the ground meat does not need to be tenderized.

Jambalaya, Creole-Style

It is hard to think of a dish that is so easy to make that is also so incredibly tasty! This is the opposite side of the spectrum from comfort food. This Cajun-Creole classic is for people who enjoy intensely flavored food. The only possible difficulty is not in the actual preparation of the dish but the obtaining of the *andouille* sausage, a spicy smoked pork product that contributes a tremendous amount of the flavor to this dish. At one time, it was almost unavailable outside of New Orleans; now it is available in many metropolitan area specialty food stores along with *chorizo*, a similar product used in Spanish (think *paella*) and Mexican dishes. For those who live in areas where this product is not available, there is always online or mail order.

One of the other great Cajun-Creole family of dishes are the gumbos. While these are equally delicious, the requirement for a dark roux (a long cooked fat and flour mixture which can become dangerously hot) makes these dishes less suitable for beginning cooks.

Jambalaya has a lot of basic similarities to Rice Pilaf, another one of the recipes in this book. In that dish, we cook raw rice in some fat to keep the grains separate and then add a flavorful liquid to cook the rice. Jambalaya being a main dish has a lot more flavorings in the form of *andouille* sausage which when its fat is rendered, spreads its spicy seasoning throughout the dish along with whatever meats and/or seafood the cook chooses. Like chili con carne, every cook's version is at least a little bit different from all the others.

But there are some common ingredients to almost all jambalayas other than the rice. One is the use of a base combination of aromatic vegetables, onions, celery, and bell pepper referred to by Cajun and Creole cooks as the "holy trinity". In fact this combination shows up so often in Cajun/Creole cooking that a cook can almost start with it and then decide what dish to make! (This is a variation of the more universally used vegetable base combination called a *mirepoix* which consists of two parts onions to one part each of carrots and celery.) The *andouille* sausage has a smoky and spicy flavor that is a must for making an authentic jambalaya. As mentioned above, it is more widely available but if you cannot find it, a hot smoked sausage will do in a pinch. For those who do not care for spicy food (if you are still reading this), a regular smoked sausage or just ham can be used.

As mentioned after the recipe, this Creole style uses tomatoes where the Cajun version would probably not. For those who want a more intensely tomato flavored dish, the tomato paste is offered as an option. I personally prefer the version without the paste so the tomatoes blend in with all of the other great flavors this dish has to offer without overpowering them.

Ingredients	*Procedure*
• 3 tablespoons butter, salted • ¾ cup onions, chopped • ¾ cup celery, chopped • ¾ cup green bell pepper, chopped • 2 teaspoons kosher salt	1. In a large sauce pot over medium high heat, sauté the onions, celery, bell pepper, and salt until very lightly browned, about 5–8 minutes.
• ½ pound andouille sausage, cut lengthwise and then into ¼ inch thick slices • ½ pound ham steak, cut into ¼ inch cubes (or use 1 pound of ham if omitting andouille)	2. Stir in the andouille and ham and brown well.
• 1 tablespoon dried basil • 2 cloves garlic, chopped finely • ¼ teaspoon ground cloves	3. Stir in the basil, garlic and cloves and sauté for about 2 minutes.
• 1 cup long grain white rice, uncooked	4. Add the rice and mix well, being sure to coat the rice with the other ingredients. Sauté this mixture for about 5 minutes or until the rice begins to brown just slightly.

Ingredients	*Procedure*
• 1 (13 ounce) can stewed tomatoes • 1 (6 ounce) can tomato paste (optional) • 1 (15 ounce) can reduced sodium chicken broth or water	5. Add the tomatoes (break them up with a spoon), optional tomato paste, and chicken broth; simmer covered for 30 minutes.
• 1 pound raw shrimp, peeled and deveined	6. At this point, the cooking liquid should be almost absorbed by the rice. Taste and correct seasonings, adding salt and/or cayenne pepper to taste (it will already be hot from the andouille so make sure and taste first). Add the shrimp and simmer covered until the rice is tender, about 10 minutes.
• ¼ cup green onions, chopped • ¼ cup Italian flat leaf parsley, chopped	7. Remove from the heat and let stand, covered, until all of the liquid is absorbed by the rice, about 10 minutes. Mix in the green onions and parsley and serve. SERVES 4–6.

A few more words...

Q. What is a Cajun or Creole?

A. Food that is indigenous to Louisiana is often called Cajun or Creole cooking.

Cajuns migrated to the New Orleans area from Acadia, Nova Scotia from where they were exiled by the British. Many of these Acadians settled in the rural waterways and bayous outside the city. Their cooking has a French influence and makes use of a lot of seafood that is widely available there. It is a simple hearty food without pretensions.

Creoles are long time inhabitants of the New Orleans area. The people and the food have been shaped by immigrants from France, Spain, and Africa along with the Native American population. Their food has a more sophisticated restaurant style. The use of butter (instead of oil) along with the tomatoes in this jambalaya is what would most likely identify this as Creole style rather than Cajun.

But over time the differences between these cuisines has become more technical than practical. This is why Cajun chef Paul Prudhomme decided to just refer to it all as Louisiana cooking in his fine book *Chef Paul Prudhomme's Louisiana Kitchen* which is a great source for those interested in learning more about this style of cooking.

Grilled Steak

Using a gas or charcoal grill this is a simple dish to prepare. But to end up with a tender and juicy steak, there are a few details one first needs to learn.

- *Which cuts of meat are tender and which are tough?*

- *Which cuts of meat are more juicy and which tend to be more dry?*

- *What is USDA inspection and grading all about? What's the difference between Prime, Choice and Select grades?*

- *What is the best equipment and technique for cooking a great steak?*

More fat <<<<<<<<<——————————————>>>>>>>>>>>More lean

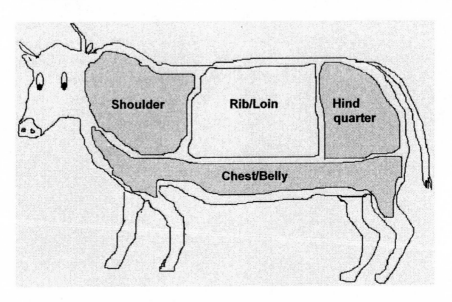

The muscles that work hardest are the weight bearing ones shown in Gray .

- On this steer which for our example is typical for all four legged animals, the areas shown in gray work the hardest and therefore yield the *tough cuts of meat*. The rib/loin area does the least amount of work which yields *tender cuts of meat*.

- The note on the top of the diagram refers to the relative fat distribution in the animal. More fat in the muscles of the animal (marbling) yields a *more juicy cut of meat* when cooked. Less fat results in a *less juicy cut of meat*.

  It is important to note that the type and length of cooking can greatly affect how tender and juicy the end product is! More on that later…

Since we want to learn more about this piece of beef, let's talk about specifics concerning beef.

Beef—Primal Cuts *(labeled below in italics)*

More fat <<<<<<<<<————————————>>>>>>>>>>More lean

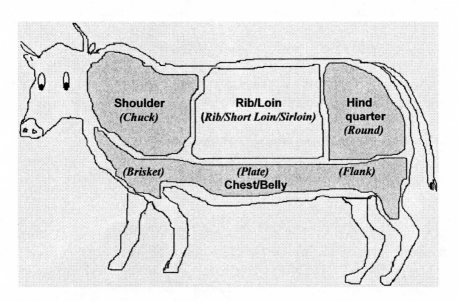

OK, our steer is back but this time, there are some additional names (*in italics*) next to our generic four legged animal anatomy names. These are the meat industry standardized names for these parts of the steer known as **primal cuts**.

But we as retail consumers don't purchase beef as primal cuts; we purchase individual cuts like T-bone steak, rump roast and the like which are parts of the primal cuts. What's the point of learning about primal cuts? Two points—one, knowing the primal cut your retail cut of beef comes from will tell you a lot about how tender the cut is and how it needs to be cooked to get satisfactory results. *As a reminder, the white area on the steer above has the tender cuts; the gray areas are the tough cuts.* Secondly, the different names of the retail cuts can be confusing. The same retail cut of beef can have different names in different regions of the country. But the name of the primal cut it comes from is an industry standard familiar to butchers everywhere. *Note: because the pig has a somewhat different anatomy from a steer, the names of its primal cuts are different—more on that later in the Appendix.*

To help consumers, more retail sellers of beef are labeling their beef with both the name of the primal and retail cut. Examples: Short Loin-T-Bone Steak; or Round-Rump Roast. Some sellers can be vague about what they are selling. For example, if strips of beef are packaged and labeled only as 'Beef for Stroganoff', how do you know how tender it will be? The answer is you don't! It can be from the round or somewhere on the loin which would make a world of difference. If you are considering a particular cut of meat and don't know what primal cut it comes from, ask the butcher. It's his or her job to know meat and the basics on how a particular cut is best cooked. If you can't find someone knowledgeable to talk to where you shop, maybe you should shop elsewhere even if it means paying a little more.

For those who would like to learn more about primal and retail meat cuts, see *Beef—A Geographic Tour* and *Pork—A Geographic Tour* in the Appendix.

Now that we are at the store looking at the meat display…

- *What is USDA inspection and grading all about? What's the difference between Prime, Choice and Select grades?*

All meat sold in the U.S. <u>must</u> be inspected by the United States Department of Agriculture to ensure that it is wholesome and fit for human consumption.

In addition, the USDA offers an <u>optional</u> grading service paid for by the meat producer that inspects beef for overall eating quality. As mentioned before, more fat in the muscles of the animal (marbling) yields a more juicy cut of meat when cooked. In addition this marbling contributes to flavor and tenderness.

The *USDA Prime* grade has the most marbling. However, it is scarce as only about 2% of the beef produced has this grade. Most of the available Prime meat goes to upscale steakhouses and hotels. The few retail sellers who offer it charge an arm and a leg which reflects this scarcity. While Prime is unquestionably excellent beef, most people would agree that Choice grade beef (see below) is a better buy for the buck.

 The *USDA Choice* grade has ample marbling but not as much as Prime. This is the standard offering of most meat retailers. Unfortunately, because of recent revisions in the USDA grading standards, the amount of marbling in Choice meat can vary considerably. This is more important in selecting a tender steak to grill than say, for meat to use in a stew. Some stores are now marketing different brand names of Choice beef to identify their product as being on the high end of the Choice grade. A good relationship with the butcher where you shop will help you sort this all out.

 The *USDA Select* grade has little or no marbling. Once again, this is more important in selecting a tender steak to grill than for meat to use in a stew. Indeed, many institutions would probably use this grade of beef to make stews.

A few retailers sell ungraded or *no roll* beef as it is called within the industry. Without the help of a USDA grade for the beef, you are on your own. Chances are, most of this beef would rate a Select grade if the producer was willing to pay for the grading.

• *What is the best equipment and technique for cooking a great steak?*

Since a cut of beef we would get from the rib or loin area of the steer is already tender, we are cooking to develop a great tasting brown crust on the outside of the steak while not overcooking the inside to the point where it becomes dry. This means a high heat dry cooking method. However, high heat cooking methods for steak also guarantee a lot of smoke and grease vapor in the air. While this makes for a pleasant aroma when cooking outdoors, it can make for an unpleasant mess inside the house unless a kitchen is equipped with an adequate ventilation system that pulls the smoke outside—most are not. So this recipe is based on cooking on an outdoor grill.

The two main types of grills are gas and charcoal fueled. Each has its own advantages and disadvantages.

- *Gas grills* are becoming a more and more popular choice for people who want an efficient and convenient way to enjoy the taste of outdoor grilling. They light easily in all but the coldest weather and maintain a steady amount of heat without all the fussing required with charcoal. However, gas grills are more expensive to buy than charcoal grills and according to the charcoal advocates, don't impart quite as much smoky flavor to the food as charcoal.

- *Charcoal grills* can cook at higher temperatures (about 600°F for charcoal briquettes and about 700°F for lump charcoal compared to about 500°F for most gas grills) which makes it easier to obtain the nice seared crust we want on a steak. However, charcoal grills require a lot of active management by adding coals to keep it at a steady temperature—a disadvantage especially if a longer cooking time is required. But charcoal grills are truly portable for when the occasion demands a cookout away from home.

The verdict is that charcoal wins with the purists who want the best taste possible and are willing to devote the extra effort that charcoal cooking requires. But gas grills are undeniably convenient and a winner with those who admire its practicality.

The following recipe is about as simple as it gets. The beef cuts selected are from the tender Rib/Loin area of the animal so they are naturally tender. All we need to do is apply some high heat to brown the outside and avoid overcooking the inside of the steak. The oil applied to the steak acts as a heat conductor allowing it to brown quicker. The coarse kosher salt crystals applied to the steak before cooking become part of the outer seared crust and contribute much more to the steak's flavor than just adding salt at the table to an unseasoned steak. The estimated cooking times are based on the heat of the grill and the thickness of the steak. In general, it is far better to cook to particular internal temperatures than by time guidelines but steaks are too thin to allow the practical use of a meat thermometer. A little practice will give you a good feel for how long to cook the steak to your desired doneness.

Ingredients	*Procedure*
• Rib-eye, T-bone, or Porterhouse steak, about ¾–1" thick* • Vegetable oil to lightly coat • Kosher salt	1. Leave the steak out at room temperature for about a half hour while lighting the charcoal or gas grill. When the grill attains its maximum heat, lightly coat each side of the steak with the vegetable oil and then sprinkle a generous amount of kosher salt on each side. 2. Place the steak on the hot grill. Gas grills usually require the cover to be used to cook at the required high heat. After about 4 minutes, check underneath for a brown crust and juices starting to seep out the top of the steak. At that point, turn the steak over and cook about 2 minutes more for medium rare, 3 minutes for medium and 4 minutes for medium well. (These times are approximate and will vary based on grill temperatures; when in doubt, undercook and place back on the grill if necessary.) 3. Allow the steak to rest for at least a couple of minutes before cutting into it to keep most of the juices inside the steak when it is cut. SERVING—1 STEAK PER PERSON

* An excellent alternative is a ¾–1" thick pork chop which when grilled this way tastes just about the same as a beef steak but for as little as one third the price. Just be sure not to grill past medium well leaving the inside a light shade of pink to keep the chop tender and juicy.

A few more words...

In general, dry cooked meats and vegetables that require salt usually benefit from sprinkling the salt on right before cooking instead of after (but not too long before cooking or the juices will be drawn out by the salt). The course crystals in kosher salt make it easier to sprinkle evenly on the food surfaces than table salt with its very fine particles which is why many cooks standardize on kosher salt except for uses like salting water for boiling where regular table salt is just fine. Anytime you decide to substitute table salt for kosher salt when called for, you will need to use about a third less by volume because of its denser structure.

Grilled Chicken

Grilling chicken is similar to grilling steak except for two main differences. One is that chicken must be cooked through until the juices run clear but the white meat of the breast which has less fat than the dark meat should not be overcooked or it will quickly dry out. The other is that unlike steak which is seared at high heat to get a flavorful crust, chicken needs more careful management of the heat level to keep the outside from burning before the inside cooks through. To help keep the chicken moist and flavorful, here is a recipe using a Greek style marinade using olive oil and lemon juice. It is also excellent on grilled pork or lamb. When you go to a Greek food festival to eat *souvlakia*, which is pork or lamb shish kebab, a marinade like this is what they likely use to prepare this dish.

The instructions tell us to cook the chicken until it is nicely browned all over. But because we are dealing with chicken, nicely browned all over is not necessarily cooked through. Experienced grill cooks can usually judge by eye when the chicken pieces are cooked. For the beginner, the best way is to use the instant read thermometer making sure the tip of the probe is not touching any bone. Remove when the breasts are at 155°F and all other pieces are at 165–170°F internal temperature. The chicken will continue to cook a bit more when resting on the serving platter.

Ingredients	*Procedure*
Marinade: • ½ cup extra virgin olive oil • Juice of 2 lemons or about ¼ cup bottled lemon juice • 1 tablespoon dried oregano • 1 teaspoon kosher salt • 1 teaspoon freshly ground pepper • 2 cloves garlic minced or about 1 tablespoon garlic powder	1. Mix the marinade in a gallon sized zipper top plastic bag.

Ingredients	*Procedure*
• 3 pounds chicken, cut into serving pieces	2. Place the chicken pieces in the bag and after squeezing out as much air as possible, seal the bag and place in the refrigerator for about 2–3 hours.
	3. Place the chicken on a medium hot grill, turning as each side browns. The oil will likely cause some flare-ups so it is important to keep an eye on the chicken and keep turning and moving it to make sure it doesn't burn. Cook until nicely browned all over.
	4. If the chicken still needs more cooking inside after it is browned (most likely the dark meat), move the pieces to a cooler part of the grill to finish cooking. If the surface of the chicken appears to be drying out, baste occasionally with the leftover marinade to keep the chicken moist—but for safety, make sure the marinade on the surface of the chicken has a chance to heat through before removing it. Discard all leftover marinade after cooking.
	SERVES 4

A few more words...

Dry rubs like what is used on the spare ribs and marinades like the one used here are some of the most effective ways to boost the flavor of food.

Marinades normally include the following:

- An acid ingredient like lemon juice, vinegar, or even yogurt. This acid penetrates the surface of the food, providing flavor.

- An oil to keep the food moist during marinating and later on during cooking. It can be a neutral flavored vegetable oil or an extra virgin olive oil if we want that flavor present.

- Seasonings like herbs and spices to provide additional flavor. It helps that fat (in this case, oil) is a wonderful vehicle for distributing all of these flavorings throughout the surface of the food.

Note that we are talking about the surface of the food. The acid in the marinade only penetrates the surface of the food to provide flavor. We do not let it penetrate deep into the food to try and tenderize it. That would turn the meat into an unappetizing mushy texture. One of the most common meats that are marinated is beef flank steak for London broil. Although the end product is tasty because of the marinade, it is only made tender enough by first of all not cooking it beyond medium rare and then by slicing very thinly 'across the grain' or in other words, across the long muscle fibers so it doesn't turn out tough and stringy.

Roast Prime Rib of Beef au Jus

Still another tender cut of meat but this time we will use the oven for another dry heat method to roast this cut to juicy perfection. Admittedly, this particular cut is an expensive one that is mostly for special occasions but it is still a great dish to have in the repertoire because few dishes are so effortless that produce such special results. In addition, fewer restaurants are offering this dish anymore and those that do, tend to do an indifferent job of it by overcooking it to an unappetizing gray color. To avoid overcooking, it is vital to use either an instant read thermometer to periodically check the internal temperature or better yet, use a digital thermometer placed outside the oven which has a cable connection to a probe that is placed inside the meat. Once the meat reaches a selected internal temperature, an alarm alerts the cook to remove the roast.

Roasting is one of the simplest and most efficient ways to cook a tender cut of meat. Unlike cooking over the direct heat of a stove burner or grill which can burn the meat while leaving the inside undercooked, roasting in an oven heats the air around the meat which in turn gently cooks it. This results in more even cooking where less can go wrong in a hurry. Unless very high oven temperatures are used, the only thing that can really go wrong is overcooking to the point of dryness. Using a probe thermometer with an alarm keeps this from happening.

By the way, there is no appreciable difference between *roasting* and *baking*. Most meat cooked in the oven is considered to be roasted as opposed to breads, cakes, and pies which are baked. OK, meat loaf is baked but that's an exception. The point is that the cooking technique is the same; it's just a matter of semantics.

Since roasting is a dry heat method, it stands to reason that the cut of meat had better have an ample amount of fat or it is likely to dry out. The best cut of all from the four legged animals for this purpose is from the rib section which is the fattiest part of the tender section of the animal. In beef, this is called a standing rib roast which if cut into steaks would be rib steaks or if the rib bone is removed, rib-eye steaks. This roast is more often called a prime rib roast, a name that is a bit misleading because most households and even restaurants serve USDA Choice beef instead of Prime. But because this is the name by which it is most well known, it is used here too.

Really good prime rib unless it is a well done end cut will have an even pink or reddish interior all the way through when it is carved. In addition, it will be equally juicy from the outside edge all the way into the center of each cut. The only way to accomplish this is to roast the meat at a steady low temperature. Many restaurants that serve prime rib have special prime rib ovens where the roasts are cooked slowly at as little as 200°F for maybe 4 or 5 hours until coming up to rare or medium rare. Once cooked, they are held in the oven to stay warm until they are sliced to order. The rare or medium rare orders just need slicing and a ladle of *jus* and they are ready to go. For customers ordering their rib roast cooked more, a few minutes under a hot broiler will do the trick.

Since these techniques work reliably for restaurants, it only makes sense for the home cook to adopt these methods too. A prime rib oven is not necessary; the home oven will do just fine. But since many home ovens cannot accurately regulate such a low temperature setting as 200°F, a temperature of 250°F is recommended which accomplishes about the same results and reduces the cooking time for those of us who are not professionals preparing for the evening's diners. Another procedure that helps to ensure even cooking through the roast is to keep it out a room temperature for about an hour before roasting to allow the center to come up to near room temperature.

A roasting pan is not even necessary unless it is an especially large roast. A large sauté pan with a metal handle and without a non-stick coating will do just fine. The rib bones on the bottom of the roast serve as a natural rack to keep the meat above the cooking juices which will keep it roasting instead of stewing in those juices.

The sauté pan does two other duties. Because little or no browning occurs at these low temperatures, the meat can be made more appealing by rubbing a little vegetable oil and sprinkling some kosher salt on it similar to the procedure for preparing a steak and then browning the outside of the roast on the stovetop. The caramelized drippings left in the sauté pan will then contribute to the making of a delicious *jus* that you can ladle over the finished roast just like the restaurants do.

Ingredients	*Procedure*

• 1 standing rib roast (usually including 3 or 4 rib bones)
 	
• Vegetable oil for coating
 	
• Kosher salt for sprinkling on the roast
	1. Remove the roast from the refrigerator about an hour before roasting. Preheat the oven to 250°F.
	
	2. Rub a little vegetable oil on the outside of the roast (except the bottom between the ribs) and sprinkle a light but even layer of kosher salt over the oiled roast. Heat in the sauté pan over medium high heat and using a large pair of tongs turn the roast so that it browns on all sides (once again, except the bottom of the roast between the rib bones).
	
	3. When the roast is evenly browned all over, stick the probe from the thermometer so that the tip is in the center of the roast not touching fat or bone (which would result in a false reading).
	
	4. Set the alarm on the thermometer unit to:
	  i. 120°F for rare
	  ii. 130°F for medium rare
	  iii. 140°F for medium
	  iv. 150°F for medium well
	
	5. Base the alarm setting on the lowest doneness desired on one of the slices and place the remaining slices under a broiler after roasting for those who want their serving cooked more. Do not use a microwave for this purpose; it will give the meat a steamed flavor. The end cuts of the roast lend themselves particularly well for those who want their meat more well done. Depending on the oven and the size of the roast, the roasting time will be about 2½ to 3 hours.

Ingredients	*Procedure*
• 2 shallots, chopped fine • ¼ cup white wine • 1–15oz. can of reduced sodium beef broth • Salt or pepper to taste	6. When it is done, remove the roast (remember, the handle is hot!) to a cutting board to rest while making the *jus* in the sauté pan as follows. Spoon out and discard any excess pools of fat in the drippings at the bottom of the pan. About a tablespoon of fat left over is about right. Over medium high heat on the stovetop, add the chopped shallots and sauté until softened but not brown. Add the wine and with a wooden spoon, scrape off any browned meat drippings stuck on the bottom of the pan. Add the beef broth and reduce to a simmer for about 10 minutes. Pour through a strainer (to remove the shallots) into a gravy boat or similar container. Add salt or pepper if needed. (The beef broth is already salty so additional salt is probably not necessary.) 7. The best way to carve is to remove the beef with a serrated knife (preferably an electric knife) along the inside of the rack of bones. The resulting boneless roast can then be sliced as desired.

A few more words...

Q. So why not roast a boneless rib roast to begin with?
A. Roasting any meat on the bone helps to preserve juiciness. Cuts with the bones removed expose more of the meat's surface to drying out from the heat of roasting.

Q. What other meats are good for roasting?
A. As mentioned before, the rib section is the best for roasting because of its tenderness and ample amount of fat—but it is the most expensive. Rack of lamb is the equivalent of the rib roast for beef. It can be browned in a sauté pan just like the beef rib roast and then placed in the oven (with the probe thermometer) to finish cooking. The rib section for pork is usually used for pork chops but it too can be roasted. However, because pork has less fat than beef or lamb, drying out is always a concern so it is recommended not to cook it beyond a 155°F internal temperature which will leave the meat a little pink in the center.

Chicken and turkey are classic candidates for roasting. But because of the different cooking requirements for white meat (the breast) and the dark meat, cooking whole birds presents difficulties for the beginning cook that are best avoided. Roasting pieces of poultry at 350°F brushed with a little butter or olive oil and salt/pepper gives the cook enough control to remove the white meat at a 155°F internal temperature keeping it juicy while leaving the dark meat to cook through at 170°F using an instant read thermometer to check. Whole turkey breasts instead of the whole turkey make cooking a Thanksgiving turkey easy enough for the beginner and truth be known, most people prefer the white meat anyhow.

Sautéed Pork Medallions in a Pan Sauce

Like the grilled steak, this is a tender cut of meat. Because of their more manageable size, these are more suited to cooking on the stovetop. But to do it properly requires a sauté pan that does NOT have a non-stick surface. This kind of pan collects caramelized drippings from browning the meat and allows us to make a pan sauce to spoon over top of the finished meat. What's the big deal about a pan sauce? A pan sauce is the quickest way for the inexperienced cook to create something that tastes so good it is something that one would only expect to find at a fine restaurant. Once you taste it, you will be amazed at what you created which hopefully, will whet your appetite to learn more and keep amazing yourself! (not to mention your friends and family who will get to taste your creations)

Just about any relatively thin boneless cut of meat is suitable for this cooking method. Boneless chicken breast and veal are classic choices. But for this dish, we are using pork medallions which are crosswise cuts of the pork tenderloin from ¾ to 1 inch thick. Pork tenderloins are available in just about every supermarket often wrapped in plastic with a marinade like teriyaki to enhance its flavor. These are the tender equivalents of the beef tenderloin (filet) but at a fraction of a cost compared to beef. But just like the beef tenderloin what it excels at in tenderness, it is a bit lacking in flavor because it comes from a part of the animal that is less exercised and is low in fat.

Cooking the pork tenderloins whole after marinating or brushing sauce on them addresses the flavor issue somewhat. But when the cooked meat is cut for serving, the cross sections are relatively tasteless because they were not exposed to any of the browning or marinating. The method suggested here is to cut the pork tenderloin into slices before cooking. This way the cross sectional area gets browned on both sides and can absorb some of the resulting pan sauce.

Pan sauces are made by taking advantage of the caramelized meat drippings that are stuck on the bottom of the pan from sautéing the meat.

- After the meat is removed to a separate serving platter, shallots and often garlic are lightly sautéed to add flavor to the sauce. (Shallots, a mild-mannered member of the onion family provide a more subtle sophisticated flavor than onions but onions will do in a pinch.)

- Then some kind of alcohol like wine or brandy is used as a flavorful solvent to help dissolve the meat drippings on the bottom of the pan to incorporate their flavor into the sauce. Then most of the alcohol is boiled off since we usually want the flavor of the alcoholic beverage but not its burn on the tongue. *Safety note*—when adding distilled spirits with a higher alcohol content like brandy or rum, you should first remove the pan from the heat to avoid possible injury from igniting the liquid.

- Then liquids like chicken broth and fats like butter or cream are added to finish the sauce. Unsalted butter as used here gives us more precise control over the amount of salt added. Unlike gravies that use flour as a thickener, the sauce is thickened and the flavors are intensified by boiling off the excess water.

Don't let the technical explanation make this seem more complicated than it is. Once you have done a pan sauce once or twice, you will be able to turn them out effortlessly.

Ingredients	*Procedure*
• 2 whole pork tenderloins (about 1½ pounds total) • Kosher salt as required • Freshly ground black pepper as required	1. Preheat the oven to 200°F. 2. Remove the silverskin, a shiny sinewy covering on the tenderloin by slipping a pointed paring knife blade just under it and running down the length of the filet, peeling it off. Cut the tenderloins into ¾ to 1 inch thick slices (medallions). Lightly pound the medallions with a meat pounder or the side of a chef's knife to flatten into shape. Blot the medallions on paper toweling to remove any excess moisture and then season them on each side with salt and pepper.

Ingredients	Procedure
• 1 tablespoon unsalted butter • 1 tablespoon vegetable oil	3. Using medium high heat, melt the butter in a large sauté pan and add oil; swirl together occasionally until the fat mixture becomes hot and begins to turn a light brown. 4. Lay the medallions in the pan and sauté about 2–3 minutes on each side until they are nicely browned. Add a little oil and butter if the fat looks like it is starting to burn. The pork is done when it becomes slightly firm to the touch. Do not overcook or the meat will become tough and dry! Remove and set aside on a serving platter and place in the 200°F oven to stay warm while preparing the sauce. (Alternatively, the cooked medallions can be returned to the finished sauce to warm thorough before serving.)
• 2 large shallots, minced (about ¼ cup) • 1 clove garlic, minced • ½ cup dry white wine • ¾ cup reduced sodium chicken broth	5. Add the shallots and sauté until softened, about 1 minute. 6. Add the garlic and sauté until fragrant, about ½ minute. 7. Add the wine and then raise the heat to high. Boil until evaporation reduces the liquid by one half, scraping the brown residue from the bottom of the pan with a wooden spoon. 8. Add the broth and any accumulated juices from the pork and boil to a thin syrupy mixture, about 4–5 minutes. Remove from heat.

Ingredients	Procedure
• 2 tablespoons unsalted butter, cut into pieces and softened • 1 lemon to provide freshly squeezed juice • Chopped parsley for garnish	9. To finish the sauce, scatter the butter pieces and stir lightly until they just melt. Add about a tablespoon of lemon juice. Taste and correct seasonings, adding salt, pepper or more lemon juice to taste. 10. Pour the finished pan gravy over the medallions, garnish with a sprinkling of chopped parsley and serve immediately. SERVES 3 TO 4.

A few more words...

- The lemon juice is a very important flavor addition to the sauce. Adding acids like lemon juice or vinegar cuts through the richness of some foods and brightens the flavor.

- Especially for the beginning cook, it is a good idea to keep jargon out of the recipe. However, for those who wish to learn more from other cook books and magazines, running into jargon is almost inevitable since experienced cooks use this to try and convey recipe instructions efficiently. There, you may run into terms like *fond* for the caramelized meat drippings that stick to the bottom of the pan and *deglazing* for the process of using the wine to dissolve those drippings to incorporate their wonderful flavor into the sauce.

- You will find that the finished sauce is not as thick as flour thickened gravy but not as thin as a *jus* poured over prime rib. Swirling the butter cubes in at the end and just allowing them to barely melt accomplishes this. This is a French technique in sauce making called *monter au beurre* or loosely, mounting the butter. Hey, I didn't make this stuff up!

- If you read enough of what I write, you will detect an agenda against overcooking meat that is tender to begin with. The pork medallions are intended to come out a faint pink in the center after cooking. The time given to cook them on each side is a best guess based on the thickness of the medallions and the amount of heat used. Also keep in mind that keeping the meat warm in the oven or warming it in the sauce will continue the cooking somewhat so slightly underdone will work out OK. As it starts to cook on the inside, the meat will start to become progressively more firm when pressing a finger into it. When the meat is raw on the inside, it has a squishy feel. When it is well done, it is noticeably firm to the touch. Experienced cooks use this gradual increase in firmness to help judge how much a piece of meat that they are cooking is done. For the less experienced, cutting a corner off to take a peek inside is perfectly OK or if presentation is important, use an instant read thermometer inserted into the center from the side. It should read about 155°F after the tip of the thermometer probe is inserted in the center for about 10 seconds. For those who want well done, the choice is always yours but since pork tenderloin is exceptionally lean, it will dry out and toughen pretty quickly with more cooking.

Breaded Cutlets

With so many meat dishes that can be cooked on the stove top, it is difficult to pick one to represent the group. Breading and pan frying different kinds of meat (and seafood) is popular in many parts of the world because if cooked properly, the breading is crispy and tasty and the contents inside which are shielded from direct heat stay moist—as long as the food is not overcooked. Indeed breaded, pan fried food is so good whether it's chicken breast cutlets or perhaps breaded pork chops, breaded fish, breaded veal cutlets, or even chicken fried steak. This makes it worthwhile for all cooks to make what is known by chefs as the '*standard breading procedure*' a part of their cooking arsenal.

The 'standard breading procedure' consists of three steps:

- The item to be breaded is dipped in **flour** until there is a thin coating covering the entire surface. Any extra is shaken off.

- Then the floured item goes into an **egg wash**, essentially a beaten egg with perhaps a little water or milk added if needed to ensure enough liquid to moisten all of the pieces. When the flour and egg are combined in this way it acts as a strong adhesive for the final coating. Many recipes omit the flour step and simply use the egg wash and the final coating. This tradeoff makes the procedure a little less messy but the outside coating doesn't stick quite as well.

- Then the item is ready for the **final coating**. For this dish, we are using seasoned bread crumbs but you may decide that the more neutral flavoring of unseasoned crumbs is more to your taste. For fried chicken, the final coating can be crushed corn flakes or even another dip in flour. Some recipes call for freshly made bread crumbs with or without seasoning which creates a different texture in the finished dish. If you wish, you can experiment with different choices to find out what you like best.

Once the food is breaded, it is then pan fried in oil until browned nicely on both sides. Extra virgin olive oil provides a bit more flavor but vegetable oil works OK too. If the meat is cut and then pounded until it is thin, this will be enough to be able to cook it through to be ready to eat. If the meat is not cooked enough from the pan frying process, placing it in a 350°F oven to finish cooking will do the trick. Using a probe thermometer in the meat connected to an external temperature readout will help us reach the correct final internal temperature without overcooking.

For the 'thin' example we will use chicken cutlets that are made from chicken breast cut and pounded to a thickness of about ¼ inch. This same recipe will work interchangeably with turkey breast cutlets or veal scaloppini cutlets (slices from the rear leg).

Ingredients	*Procedure*
• 2 boneless, skinless chicken breasts • Kosher salt and freshly ground pepper	1. Cut the chicken breasts lengthwise down the center and then use a meat pounder to flatten each piece to about ¼ inch thick. Sprinkle lightly with kosher salt and fresh ground pepper. Lightly press the kosher salt and pepper into the surface of the chicken.
Breading ingredients: • ½ cup flour • 1 egg, beaten • 1 cup seasoned bread crumbs	2. Prepare the breading ingredients by lining up (in order) a 1 quart zip top bag with the flour, a pie plate or shallow bowl with the beaten egg, and another 1 quart zip top bag with the bread crumbs next to each other. 3. To do the breading, place a piece of chicken in the flour, close the bag and shake until it is coated evenly. Shake off any excess flour back into the bag. Lay both sides of the flattened chicken breast into the beaten egg until covered. Finally, place the piece of chicken in the bag with the bread crumbs. Close it and shake until the crumbs evenly cover the chicken. Repeat for each piece of chicken and replenish flour, egg, or bread crumbs if required. The breading can be done an hour ahead of the pan frying with the chicken pieces being placed separately on wax paper in the refrigerator.

Ingredients	*Procedure*
• About ¼ cup extra virgin olive oil (or vegetable oil) for pan frying • Freshly squeezed lemon juice and/ or horseradish sauce	4. Heat the oil over medium high heat, and then add the chicken pieces. Turn when they become a medium brown color. Be careful not to let the breading burn. Brown the second side and then remove to a serving dish. A squirt of freshly squeezed lemon juice or perhaps some horseradish sauce would be a great finishing touch.

For those who wish to progress a step further…and create chicken (or veal or turkey) Parmesan, omit the lemon juice or horseradish and place the finished cutlets in a baking dish. Pour some marinara sauce over the cutlets. You can use either commercially prepared sauce for simplicity or use the following ingredients selected from the Tomato Sauce recipe and follow the preparation instructions there.

- • 3 tablespoons extra virgin olive oil
- • 1 medium onion, chopped finely
- • 2 cloves of garlic, minced
- • 1 teaspoon dried basil
- • ½ cup dry white wine

- • 28 oz. can Italian plum tomatoes packed in juice

- • Salt and freshly ground black pepper to taste
- • Red pepper flakes to taste

First sprinkle some grated Parmesan or Pecorino Romano cheese and then put some thinly sliced or shredded mozzarella (or provolone) cheese over the sauced cutlets and place under the broiler until the cheese is melted and starting to brown. Serve with additional grated cheese on the side. Pasta dressed with the remaining marinara sauce is the classic accompaniment.

A few more words...

- The technical difference between *sautéing* and *pan frying* is the amount of oil in the pan. Sautéing uses a minimal amount of oil just to coat the bottom of the pan. Pan frying uses enough oil to come up half way up the side of the food in the pan. In *deep frying* like for French fries, the food is submerged in the cooking fat.

- Other than grilling, the best way to cook a pork chop is to use this breading technique. Boneless chops about a ½ inch thick work best. This will leave the pork slightly pink in the middle and really juicy without the need for additional oven cooking. Thicker chops can be used but will likely need to be finished in the oven to be ready to eat.

- Breaded cutlets are known by different names throughout the world like *chicken Milanese* in Italy and *wiener schnitzel*, a breaded veal cutlet which is a mainstay on German restaurant menus.

Barbecued Spare Ribs

Spare ribs are a tough but flavorful part of the pig. Here, we are using a low dry heat method, barbecuing which not only tenderizes the meat but also adds additional flavor with smoke. With enough know how and the right equipment, an electric water smoker, really good barbecue is just about effortless. But since most of you don't own an electric water smoker, I have adapted the recipe for use on a covered charcoal or gas grill. It is not as convenient but if you later decide you want to barbecue a lot, then you can get the smoker. OK?

Unfortunately, the terms barbecuing and grilling are often incorrectly used interchangeably. *Grilling* is a high heat method of quickly cooking food directly over the heat source. *Broiling* is pretty much the same thing except the heat is radiated from above the food. But while grilling is great for browning an already tender cut of meat, it does nothing to improve the tenderness of a tough cut of meat like spare ribs. Here we have to use a low and slow heat source (in this case, barbecuing) to break down a tough piece of meat over a period of hours until it finally becomes tender.

But long cooking, even in liquid has a drying effect on meat. For this reason, the fattier cuts of pork like spare ribs and shoulder along with beef cuts like chuck and brisket are best suited to these methods because their internal fat along with ample connective tissue that is converted into gelatin helps to keep the meat from drying out. Trying to barbecue for example, a pork chop from the loin, a leaner part of the animal with less connective tissue would result in something looking and tasting like shoe leather. For this reason, I feel that the cooking method for baby back ribs, an already tender and drier cut from the loin is not completely interchangeable with the method for cooking spare ribs. For more information on spare ribs and other cuts of pork, see *Pork—A Geographic Tour* in the Appendix.

A smoker is the equipment of choice for barbecuing. It is little more than an enclosure with a heat source (usually charcoal or an electric element) that smolders some hardwood, and sometimes includes a water pan to provide steam to keep the smoky flavored food moist. Unlike a grill which is made to put out high heat, a well designed smoker is made to maintain a steady low temperature (about 225–250°F.) for hours on end. Either a gas or charcoal grill can be adapted to simulate a smoker as long as it has a tight fitting cover. **Since most of you don't own a smoker, I have adapted a second recipe for use on a covered charcoal or**

gas grill. It is not as convenient and doesn't turn out barbecue as good as a smoker but if you later decide you want to barbecue a lot, then you can get the smoker.

Back in 1998, I read an interesting review of smokers in *Cook's Illustrated* magazine. Based on their advice, I purchased a MECO Model 5030 electric water smoker (pictured) which I still use today and can certainly recommend. If it is not available in a store near you that sells grills and smokers, it is available online for about $125. A stainless steel version of the same smoker is available for about $225. However, keeping your smoker covered when not in use will keep it from rusting out without the extra expense for stainless steel.

Because they don't require the electric element and thermostat, charcoal smokers cost less than electric smokers. But that electric element and thermostat give you a much more steady and reliable heat source than charcoal which requires periodically adding more briquettes to keep a steady temperature. Although most barbecue purists would probably turn their nose up at using an electric smoker, **I strongly recommend electric units for those who are contemplating buying a smoker.** Once you get the hang of it, an electric water smoker effortlessly makes some pretty good barbecue.

Meanwhile, here is the recipe adapted for dual burner gas grills. To get the effect of indirect cooking, one places the ribs over the burner that is turned off and uses the other burner to provide the indirect heat. For a three burner grill, the center burner can be lit which allows ribs to be placed over the two outer burners (which are turned off and covered with drip pans or foil.)

For charcoal kettle type grills, the lit coals can be placed on one side with the ribs over a drip pan on the other side. Or if the grill is large enough, the lit coals can be placed in the center with ribs placed on the outer edges over drip pans.

To really tenderize the ribs and make them smoky tasting enough, a good 4 to 4½ hours in a smoker is required. But with the necessity of adding of frequently adding wood chips and having to use propane out of a tank, 2 to 2½ hours is a practical maximum for this gas grill method.

"Barbecued" Spare Ribs

(Recipe adapted for dual burner gas grills)

Ingredients	*Procedure*
Dry rub seasoning mix consisting of: • ½ cup (8 tablespoons) sugar • ½ cup (8 tablespoons) paprika • 1 tablespoon cayenne pepper • 1 tablespoon salt • 1 tablespoon freshly ground black pepper • 1 tablespoon garlic powder • 1 tablespoon dried thyme • 1 tablespoon dried oregano • 1 tablespoon dried basil • 1 teaspoon ground cinnamon • 1 teaspoon ground allspice • 1 teaspoon ground cardamom	1. On a piece of waxed paper, mash the dry rub ingredients together with a fork until the clumps are all dissolved.

Ingredients	Procedure
• 2 slabs St. Louis style pork ribs, each about 2¼ pounds or less • Yellow mustard for coating the ribs.	2. Coat the meaty side of the ribs with a thin layer of mustard. Sprinkle an even layer of the dry rub mixture over the mustard coating. There will be some left over for sprinkling on the ribs before serving. Set aside while the grill is prepared.
• About 2 cups hickory chips, soaked in water for at least ½ hour	3. To prepare the grill for indirect cooking, first remove the cooking grates. Place a drip pan or a sheet of aluminum foil underneath the cooking grate but on top of the burner not being used. (The ribs will be placed on this unlit side and this will capture the fat drippings rendered from the ribs to prevent flare-ups when the burner is used next time.) 4. Fire up the burner that will be used for the cooking. Sprinkle about a quarter of the soaked hickory chips through the cooking grate onto the burner. Once up to cooking temperature, replace the cover and lower the gas control to low to allow the ribs to cook slowly by indirect heat until cooked through and dark brown, about 2–2½ hours, adding wood chips about every ½ hour.

Ingredients	*Procedure*
• Barbecue sauce for final grilling and for serving on the side	5. As a finishing step, turn the gas burner to high and placed the cooked ribs on top of the heated burner, meaty side up. With enough heat, the membrane can be singed and pulled off with the tongs. Turn the ribs over about every minute or two and brush with the finishing sauce and sprinkle some leftover dry rub on the ribs before replacing the cover. Special care and attention are required at this time to make sure that the sauce browns but does not burn! Grill until the ribs are nicely browned and crispy on the outside, but not dry—no more than about 5 minutes.
	6. The slabs may be cut into individual ribs and served immediately or they can first be wrapped in aluminum foil for up to an hour or so at room temperature until ready to cut and serve. Serve with a bowl of warmed barbecue sauce on the side along with a basting brush. SERVES 4.

Real Barbecued Spare Ribs

(Recipe adapted for electric water smokers)

Ingredients	Procedure
Dry rub seasoning mix consisting of: • ½ cup (8 tablespoons) sugar • ½ cup (8 tablespoons) paprika • 1 tablespoon cayenne pepper • 1 tablespoon salt • 1 tablespoon freshly ground black pepper • 1 tablespoon garlic powder • 1 tablespoon dried thyme • 1 tablespoon dried oregano • 1 tablespoon dried basil • 1 teaspoon ground cinnamon • 1 teaspoon ground allspice • 1 teaspoon ground cardamom	1. On a piece of waxed paper, mash the dry rub ingredients together with a fork until the clumps are all dissolved.

Ingredients	Procedure
• 2 slabs St. Louis style pork ribs, each about 2¼ pounds or less • Yellow mustard for coating the ribs.	2. Coat the meaty side of the ribs with a thin layer of mustard. Sprinkle an even layer of the dry rub mixture over the mustard coating. There will be some left over for sprinkling on the ribs before serving. Set aside while the smoker is prepared.
• About 6 medium sized hickory chunks, soaked in water for at least ½ hour	3. After covering the inside of the drip bowl with heavy duty foil, fill the bowl about ¾ full with hot tap water and place in the smoker. Place 3 of the hickory chunks on the electric element. Put the ribs in the smoker, put on the cover and turn on the electricity. 4. Once up to cooking temperature, after about 2 hours of cooking, add the remaining 3 wood chunks. 5. Allow a total cooking time of about 4 to 4½ hours. The rib bones will start to protrude from the bottom of the meat which will turn a dull dark brown and finally become glossy. Turning the ribs while cooking in the smoker is not necessary.

Ingredients	Procedure
• Barbecue sauce for final grilling and for serving on the side	6. As a finishing step after smoking, fire up your gas or charcoal grill to high and place the cooked ribs directly on top of the heat source, meaty side up. With enough heat, the membrane can be singed and pulled off with the tongs. Turn the ribs over about every minute or two and brush with the finishing sauce and sprinkle some leftover dry rub on the ribs before replacing the cover. Special care and attention are required at this time to make sure that the sauce browns but does not burn! Grill until the ribs are nicely browned and crispy on the outside, but not dry—no more than about 5 minutes.
	7. The slabs may be cut into individual ribs and served immediately or they can first be wrapped in aluminum foil for up to an hour or so at room temperature until ready to cut and serve. Serve with a bowl of warmed barbecue sauce on the side along with a basting brush. SERVES 4.

A few more words...

- **Baby back ribs** can be substituted for spare ribs but should only be smoked for about 2 hours instead of 4 to keep them from drying out.

- **Chicken** parts take wonderfully to smoking and would be ready to eat in about 2 hours. Dark meat, especially wings are superb cooked this way. Chicken, like ribs benefits from a hot grilling with a little bit of sauce applied at the end of smoking to crisp up the exterior.

- A **pork butt roast** (from the shoulder) is an excellent pork barbecue alternative in place of spare ribs and will require about 4–5 hours to reach an internal temperature of 185°F using an instant read thermometer. For those who prefer beef, **brisket** is a classic choice for barbecuing in a smoker. But depending on the size of the brisket, it can take as much as 8–10 hours to reach the required internal temperature of 185°F to make it tender enough. Brisket does not need grilling after removing from the smoker.

- I keep my dry rub seasoning mix in an emptied garlic powder container. The lid keeps it fresh and the shaker top makes it easy to apply onto the ribs.

- Making ones own **barbecue sauce** isn't that difficult but with so many choices in commercially made sauces, it's probably not worth the bother. My favorite barbecue sauce is *Cattlemen's*, a long time popular foodservice brand now widely available in supermarkets to retail customers.

- **Wood chunks** are better suited to barbecue than chips since they don't burn up so quickly but chips are used for the gas grill recipe because of their more practical size. Most stores that sell grills or smokers will also sell hickory and mesquite chunks. Mesquite grilled steaks are sometimes offered by restaurants but hickory is by far the most popular wood for barbecuing pork.

- The **water pan** in the smoker does double duty by not only providing moisture by steam but also catching the fat drippings so that the separate drip pans or foil required for the grill recipes are not needed. Lining the water pan with foil before cooking will make cleanup tremendously easier.

Sole Amandine

This dish is sometimes known as 'sole almandine'; *amandine* is the French spelling. Whatever the name, this sautéed fish dish with slivered almonds, lemon juice, and finished with a simple butter sauce is delicious. Although it is a very easy dish to make, it has been mostly a restaurant dish because of the difficulty in finding fresh sole except at fish markets. Now that many supermarkets are doing a better job of stocking fresh fish, this should be a part of the home cook's repertoire for those households that enjoy fish.

This is a two part preparation which requires a pair of pans, 1 large non-stick pan for sautéing the fish and a second smaller pan or saucepot (preferably not non-stick so it is easier to keep an eye on the butter as it turns brown) for melting and browning the butter and sliced almonds to pour over the fish as a finishing sauce. The experienced cook can attend to both pans at the same time but it is perfectly OK to finish sautéing the fish before starting to melt the butter in the second pan for the finishing sauce since the hot bubbling butter will bring the fish up to serving temperature at once.

Ingredients	*Procedure*
Part one—sauté the fish • 2 sole filets • Salt and pepper • Flour for coating the fish • Vegetable oil for sautéing the fish	1. Heat a large sauté pan over medium-high heat with just enough oil to cover the bottom of the pan. 2. Salt and pepper the filets and lay them in some flour poured into a shallow plate. Be sure the flour coats both sides evenly and then be sure to shake off any excess flour.

Ingredients	*Procedure*
• Freshly squeezed lemon juice • Chopped parsley	3. Gently lay each fish filet in the hot oil flesh side down. The oil should gently bubble around the fish. Using a spatula, peek under the fish to see when it starts to turn a light golden brown. (This should take no more than a couple of minutes.) When this happens, turn the fish filets over and finish for about 1 more minute. 4. Remove to a platter or individual serving plates. Lightly blot away any visible oil on the fish or plate with a paper towel. Sprinkle the lemon juice and chopped parsley over the fish. Now proceed to the second step.
Second step—prepare the butter sauce • ½ stick butter, salted • ½ cup sliced almonds	5. Heat the butter over medium high heat. After it is melted, add the sliced almonds. Gently agitate the pan occasionally to make sure the almonds toast evenly. Carefully keep an eye on the butter and almonds as they start to turn brown. (There is a very fine line between brown and burnt!) When you can start to smell the aroma of toasted almonds, remove right away from the heat and pour the hot butter and almond mixture over the filets which will sizzle as it hits the lemon juice on the fish. Serve immediately. SERVES 2.

A few more words...

- The slivered almonds are optional; the same dish without the almonds is sole *meunière* (French for the miller's wife). The browned butter is popularly referred to by cooking professionals as *beurre noisette* (hazelnut butter).

- Any lean white fish as long as it is not too thick lends itself well to this cooking method. Trout is especially superb. Just salt and pepper and flour the trout and open it like a book, sautéing it flesh side down and then turning it over just like in the recipe for sole. The person behind the seafood counter should be able to help in selecting the right fish.

- The classic version of this recipe calls for sautéing the fish in clarified butter to give the fish more butter flavor. This requires the melted butter to have the milk solids skimmed off to keep it from burning at sautéing temperatures. Using vegetable oil simplifies the recipe without really sacrificing flavor since the butter sauce provides most of the butter flavor anyway.

Crab Cakes

The difference between good and not so good crab cakes is simple. Good crab cakes have lots of crab meat and little breading. Not so good ones are just the opposite—lots of breading and little crab meat. Many if not most restaurant versions are pretty forgettable since they have to limit the amount of expensive crab meat to be able to charge an attractive price and also make a profit. The home cook has no such constraints. Some know how in picking out the crab meat along with a good recipe that keeps the breading to the minimum amount to keep the crab cake from falling apart is all that's needed for the home cook to effortlessly produce some first rate crab cakes.

The first order of business is selecting the crab to be used. The most traditional choice is the blue crab which is commonly found in Chesapeake Bay and other places on the Atlantic Coast. Because the blue crab is so small, requiring about 8 of them to yield a pound of meat, they are usually eaten as crab cakes after someone has done the work of picking the meat out of the shells. Larger crabs like the Dungeness crab from the Pacific Coast along with the snow and king crabs from Alaska are more commonly eaten as is.

The most practical choice for most people is to purchase refrigerated, pasteurized crab meat that comes in either 8 ounce or 16 ounce containers from either seafood markets or good supermarkets that offer an assortment of fresh seafood. Much of this crabmeat is now imported from outside the United States. You can also find canned crab meat next to the canned tuna fish and salmon but the flavor and texture isn't nearly the same.

There are a number of variations for flavoring crab cakes. Some use different spice mixtures like Old Bay; some use diced peppers; some like to use a lot of heat. This recipe which I first tasted at the Grand Concourse restaurant in Pittsburgh uses very mild seasonings so the crab cakes taste like little more than just crab—nothing wrong with that!. To add a little zip, a nice mustard sauce is offered.

Not long after that, in my wanderings through the cookbook section of a local bookstore, I stumbled across *The Simply Great Cookbook* which is a collection of recipes from the kitchens of Chuck Muer, who founded a chain of seafood restaurants including the Grand Concourse mentioned above. His warm smile along with some of his beautiful food graces the cover. Although his chain of restaurants is still flourishing, Chuck was lost in a boating accident somewhere in the Bermuda Triangle. I just wish there was a way for me to thank him for sharing his wonderful recipes like these with the world.

Tony Polombo

(Recipes reprinted with permission from "The Simply Great Cookbook" by Chuck Muer
(c) 1992, Momentum Books, LLC)

Ingredients	Procedure
• 1 pound can back-fin lump crab meat, pasteurized	1. Drain the crab meat and pick through for shells and cartilage but try not to break up any of the lumps. Genuine backfin lump should have few if any shells.
• 1 egg, beaten • 5 tablespoons mayonnaise • 1 tablespoon fresh parsley, chopped • 2 teaspoons Worcestershire sauce • 1 teaspoon yellow prepared mustard • 1 teaspoon salt • ¼ teaspoon black pepper	2. In a separate bowl, mix together the ingredients listed from beaten egg through black pepper.
• ½ cup fresh bread crumbs (Tear some French or Italian bread into rough cubes and process in the blender.)	3. Gently fold the bread crumbs into the crab meat with a rubber spatula. Then gently fold the egg mixture into the crab meat. Refrigerate mixture for at least 1 hour.

Ingredients	*Procedure*
• 2 tablespoons melted butter, salted	4. Preheat the broiler.
	5. Form mixture into 8 cakes, approximately 2½ inches wide and ¾ inch thick.
	6. Place crab cakes on a foil-covered baking sheet that has been brushed lightly with melted butter. Brush the crab cakes lightly with melted butter. (At this point, they may be refrigerated until ready to broil and serve.)
	7. Broil crab cakes for 10 to 12 minutes or until golden brown on the top.

Serve 2 cakes per person. Garnish with Cold Mustard Sauce (Recipe Follows).

Cold Mustard Sauce

Ingredients	*Procedure*
• 1 cup mayonnaise • ¼ cup Dijon mustard • ½ teaspoon dry mustard • 2 teaspoons lemon juice	Combine all ingredients in a bowl and blend thoroughly. Sauce may be kept refrigerated in a covered container for up to 2 weeks.

A few more words...

Now that you have found the refrigerated, pasteurized crab meat there are other choices to make. Depending on what part of the crab the meat comes from, it can be in the form of lumps which have a wonderful texture when put into a crab cake or it can have a stringy texture which is a notch down on the desirability scale.

Refrigerated, pasteurized canned crab meat is sold in the following varieties in descending order of cost:

- *Jumbo lump* is the best of the best. Few people make crab cakes out of only jumbo lump because of its expense and difficulty in getting the large lumps to bind properly. More often, jumbo lump is used by chefs in dishes like Veal Oscar where the lumps will stand out as an important part of the presentation.

- *Backfin lump* is also an excellent product but is not as expensive as jumbo lump. *This is the crab meat that gives the best bang for the buck and is recommended above all for crab cakes.* For those who would like to create something more special and can afford it, a mixture of half jumbo lump and backfin lump fits the bill.

- *Special* consists of crab meat that is picked from the other parts of the crab's body. It is acceptable if lump crab meat is not available. But it has a more stringy texture that will make the crab cakes a little mushier without the lump meat to provide some firmness. A bigger disadvantage to *Special* is that it is more likely to have small shell fragments that have to be picked out by hand. This is a very laborious process that requires rubbing the crab meat over the fingers and palms to feel for the shell fragments. Backfin lump has little or no shells and jumbo lump should have no shells at all. (Chefs sometimes choose the more expensive jumbo lump for the tradeoff of avoiding the labor of looking for shell fragments.

- *Claw* meat which is suitable only for a preparation like crab cocktail.

Fettuccine Alfredo

It's hard to think of such a simple dish that has been botched up as often as this one. Like many Italian dishes, the secret is simply insisting on the best quality ingredients like genuine Parmigiano-Reggiano cheese to go with the heavy cream and unsalted butter. This is one of the all time great comfort foods!

One thing that makes this recipe different from many other versions is the combination of heavy cream that is thickened by boiling it down and uncooked cream that is added at the end to moisten the fettuccine and cheese. This flavor combination adds an extra dimension of flavor to the dish.

Admittedly, this dish is at its very best using freshly made pasta since it is better at absorbing the creamy sauce. But I feel that making fresh pasta is a bit too ambitious for the basic repertoire because even though it can be made completely by hand, the process is probably too laborious for most people. Therefore a food processor for mixing the dough along with pasta rolling equipment would be needed to make it practical. So the recipe calls for a commercial dried fettuccine which is more than adequate. But if you can find freshly made egg fettuccine, go for it!

Ingredients	*Procedure*
• 1 pound fettuccine	1. Boil the fettuccine in at least a gallon of water with a small handful of table salt. Use the pasta manufacturer's times on the back of the box as a guideline but be sure to test the pasta near the end of the cooking time to ensure that it is not overcooked. The cooked pasta should be tender but still have a little bit of chew left in it or as the Italians call it, *al dente.*(to the tooth). Most dried fettuccine pastas require about 10–12 minutes to cook. If using fresh pasta, the cooking time may be as little as a minute or two!

Ingredients	Procedure
• 4 tablespoons unsalted butter • 1 cup heavy cream (plus additional below) • 1 teaspoon kosher salt or to taste	2. While the pasta is cooking, melt the butter in a large sauté pan or saucepan over medium heat. Before the melted butter starts to brown, stir in the 1 cup of heavy cream. 3. Turn the heat up to medium high and allow the cream and butter mixture to boil until the cream is reduced by about half. When done reducing, it should coat the back of a spoon. Stir periodically to keep the butter and cream from separating. Add the teaspoon of kosher salt or a little more if desired just until the salt can be tasted. (The cheese will add more salt to the dish.) Keep warm on low heat until the pasta is cooked. 4. Drain the cooked pasta in a colander. After making sure all visible water is shaken and drained from the pasta, add it to the reduced cream and butter mixture.
• ¾ cup freshly grated Parmigiano-Reggiano cheese plus more for the table • ½ cup additional heavy cream (or as required)	5. Turn the heat up to medium. Stir the pasta through the cream and butter mixture to coat thoroughly. Sprinkle in a handful of the grated cheese and mix in until it starts to melt into the pasta. Repeat with additional handfuls of grated cheese. Drizzle in just enough heavy cream over the pasta to keep it from getting too dry to work with.

Ingredients	*Procedure*
• Freshly ground black pepper	6. Remove from the heat and onto a large serving platter. Sprinkle a little more cheese and stir through. Stir in a drizzle of more cream if the sauce seems a little too dry. Top off with a generous amount of freshly ground black pepper and serve immediately. Offer more grated cheese at the table.
	SERVES 3–4 AS A MAIN DISH

A few more words...

- Although this is a really rich dish, many people can and do enjoy this as an entrée but you may find this to be more appropriate as a side dish.

- I feel that genuine Parmigiano-Reggiano is needed for an authentic flavor but I have also on occasion made this with Pecorino Romano cheese as a change of pace. It is here that you can really tell the differences in the two cheeses.

- Unsalted butter is often used for sauce making because it believed by many to have a cleaner, fresher taste than regular salted butter. More importantly, it gives the cook more precise control over how much salt is in the finished dish.

- A pasta fork for stirring the pasta while cooking in the water, stirring it through the sauce and serving it on the platter really comes in handy. A sturdy plastic model is adequate.

SIDES

As stated in my introduction to Entrees, simple side dishes can fill in nicely until the cook wants to get more ambitious. Even a nice loaf of bread and perhaps a tossed salad with oil and vinegar will often complete a more than adequate meal. And since decent desserts can be purchased from bakery departments and frozen food sections, none are included here to distract you from putting most of your energy into the main dish.

But man cannot live by bread alone. Some easy rice and potato dishes (along with some information on how to buy rice and potatoes for your kitchen) are offered for the cook who is ready to add them as part of the overall meal preparation.

Excellent frozen (and to a lesser degree, canned) vegetables are widely available. While fresh ones in season are certainly desirable, the convenience of vegetables that are cut into serving pieces and blanched (briefly pre-cooked) are undeniable. Often, defrosting vegetables in the microwave and adding some butter makes a perfectly good side dish. The method given for sautéing greens in olive oil makes for a tasty side that will please just about everyone—even those who say they don't particularly care for spinach or broccoli. When fresh vegetables are is in season during the summer, one of my favorite ways to cook them is on the grill. For example, zucchini and eggplant after being sliced and brushed with some extra virgin olive oil and seasoned with salt and pepper can be grilled until they get grill marks and start to soften. The sugar that is naturally part of these vegetables starts to caramelize and develops tremendous flavors not available from most other cooking methods. Grilled asparagus done this way is especially good. And although there are many elaborate ways to grill corn on the cob, the simplest way is best. Just husk the corn and put it on a hot grill (turning occasionally) until some of the kernels start to turn an attractive shade of brown.

The creamed spinach and cream of mushroom soup are probably more for special occasions but they are easy dishes to make and are instructive for learning about sauces and cream soups.

A tossed salad is certainly nice but a Caesar salad is an elegant step up. This is a restaurant dish that is not often made by home cooks. Serve this to your guests and I will almost guarantee you they will be impressed!

Rice Pilaf

Plain steamed rice with a little butter makes an OK side dish. I make mine in the microwave using a covered casserole dish. Using the rice to water proportions on the back of the box or bag, I heat on full power for 5 minutes followed by a second heating at 30% power (defrost) for about 17 minutes. Salt and butter can be added at the beginning of cooking. Microwaves do not boil water quicker than a stovetop but it provides the advantage of automating the process.

Rice pilaf takes only a little more effort but is a quantum leap in taste. And if you know how to make rice pilaf, it is only a small step away from learning to make risotto, that wonderfully creamy Northern Italian rice dish.

Rice pilaf also lends itself to a number of flavorful additions. This recipe adds some slivered almonds toasted in a little butter to give the taste a nutty accent. In the Middle East, sweet spices like nutmeg or cinnamon are added along with possibly raisins, currants, or dried apricots. This touch of sweetness goes well with roasted meat dishes.

And adding a small handful of broken up thin spaghetti with the rice gives you a dish that Rice-a-Roni offers as a convenience food in a box.

You can experiment with any or all of these additions to see what you (and/or those you cook for) like. Or you can leave out the almonds if you just want the flavor and texture of the rice.

This is what makes cooking fun. For most of us, being able to experiment with different flavor combinations is a whole lot more interesting than just blindly following a recipe.

Ingredients	*Procedure*
• 1 tablespoon unsalted butter • ¼ cup slivered almonds • Pinch of kosher salt	1. In a small saucepan over medium high heat, melt the butter and add the almonds, sprinkling a pinch of the salt over them while allowing them to brown slightly. As soon as they start to brown, remove to a small dish and put aside until later.

Ingredients	Procedure
• 2 tablespoons unsalted butter • ½ medium onion, finely diced • Pinch of kosher salt	2. Add the 2 tablespoons of butter and once it is melted, add the onions and the pinch of kosher salt.
• 1 cup long grain white rice, uncooked	3. Once the onion start to soften, add the rice and thoroughly stir in with the butter and onions making sure that all of the rice grains are coated with the butter. Continue to cook in the butter for about another minute or so while stirring often until the butter turns a light shade of brown. Do not let the onions brown.
• 15 oz. can of reduced sodium chicken broth	4. Stir in the chicken broth and allow to come to a boil. Cover and turn the heat down to low and allow to simmer for about 15–17 minutes (without removing the lid to peek!) By this time, the rice should have absorbed just about all of the chicken broth. Remove from the heat, fluff the grains with a fork, and mix in the browned slivered almonds. Keep the lid on until ready to serve. The diner can add salt and/or black pepper or perhaps a little more butter to taste. SERVES 2–3.

A few more words...

The simplified world of rice can be divided into long grain and short grain rice. And like different types of potatoes, the main difference comes down to the amounts of starch they have.

• Long grain rice has less starch so when it is cooked, the grains stay separate. The cooked grains in long grain will clump together when refrigerated but will come apart nicely when reheated in the making of fried rice. *Parboiled* or *converted* as Uncle Ben's calls it yields rice grains that are especially good at staying separate. For the beginner who is worried about making rice that doesn't stick, this may be a good alternative even though it takes a bit longer to cook and many rice purists don't feel that it has the same pure rice flavor as conventional long grain. *Instant rice* saves time but doesn't taste as good as rice cooked from scratch.

• Short grain rice is used for dishes where the extra starch gives the dish either a creamy texture (like *arborio* rice for risotto or paella) or a purposely sticky texture (like for sushi).

Baked Potatoes

The simplest way to bake a potato is to scrub it until clean, poke a few holes in it with a fork to make sure the steam escapes and bake in a 425°F oven for about 1–1¼ hours or until the potato is tender when pressed with a finger (use a paper towel or cloth to keep from getting burned).

This is all fine but nowadays when we are often pressed for time, it would sure be nice if we could come up with a baked potato as quickly as we can, say, grill a steak. The microwave oven allows us to bake a potato in a little as 4 minutes. And it does a great job of making the inside nice and fluffy. However, the baked potato purists who want a crisp skin don't care for the soggy skin of microwaved potatoes.

I use a combination cooking method that takes advantage of the microwave's speed and the gas grill's concentrated heat to crisp up the skin. If you happen to be cooking some steaks on the grill, put the potatoes on a few minutes ahead of putting the steaks on because they will take a little more time to finish cooking. If it is not practical to light the grill, a preheated broiler will also do the trick.

Ingredients	*Procedure*
• 2—Russet or Idaho or 'baking' potatoes, about ½ pound each	1. Preheat the grill for high heat if not already using for another part of the meal.
	2. Scrub the potatoes under running water and cut away any green spots you might find. Poke some holes in the potato with a fork to allow steam to escape.
	3. Microwave the potatoes on full power for about 4 minutes per potato. Check for tenderness by pressing on the potato using a towel to keep from being burned. It should easily give in to pressure. If more cooking is required, continue to microwave for another minute and recheck for doneness.

Ingredients	*Procedure*
	4. Place the microwaved potatoes directly on the hot grill, turning every couple of minutes or so to make sure the skin gets brown and crispy evenly all over. Depending on the heat of the grill, the potatoes should be ready in about 5–7 minutes.
	5. When serving, lay the potato flat on the plate, cut a long slit down the center and carefully squeeze the ends in to allow the steam to quickly escape. Add salt, pepper, butter and/or sour cream etc. as desired.

A few more words...

There are many varieties but to try and simplify things, the world of potatoes is classified by two characteristics—either 'starchy' or 'waxy'.

- A 'starchy' potato is high in starch (of course) and low in moisture. The larger a potato grows the more starch it has and the thicker the skin is. The starchier a potato is, the mealier it is on the inside when it is cooked which makes it especially suited for baked potatoes and French fries. The large russet potatoes, a.k.a. Idaho or 'baking' potatoes are especially starchy.

- A 'waxy' potato is lower in starch and higher in moisture. Smaller potatoes sometimes called 'new potatoes' fall in this category and have thinner skins (which make it more practical to eat them without peeling). These potatoes are especially suited for roasting and potato salad where they will hold their shape as opposed to the starchy potato that would tend to disintegrate from cooking. The red potatoes and small potatoes of any kind are the least starchy.

- Everything else that doesn't fall in these extreme categories is considered an all purpose potato. For those who don't want to fuss with trying to find the ideal potato for what they are cooking, these are good enough to get by. And for mashed potatoes, any kind of potato works just as well except that red potatoes with their thinner skins are preferable for smashed potatoes where the skins are left on.

Roasted Potatoes

This is one of the easiest and tastiest potato recipes you will find. Because they are being cooked for a fairly long time in hot oil, the dried herbs may well be better than fresh ones for this dish. The slightly sweet flavor of these tiny red potatoes adds to the interest. If you cannot find the tiny 'B' sized potatoes, the larger red potatoes will also do. You will just have to cut each potato into more pieces to keep them from being too large to cook evenly.

Ingredients	*Procedure*
• 3 pounds of small 'B' size red potatoes	1. Preheat oven to 400°F. 2. Wash the potatoes under running water to remove any dirt. Do not peel. Cut the potatoes in half and then each half again in thirds, taking care to make the pieces somewhat evenly sized to ensure even cooking. Place the potato pieces in a large roasting pan.
• ½ cup extra virgin olive oil • 2 cloves garlic, minced • 2 tablespoons dried basil • 2 tablespoons dried rosemary, crumbled • 1 tablespoon kosher salt • 1 tablespoon freshly ground black pepper	3. Mix the remaining ingredients together in a small bowl with a fork and then pour over the potatoes. Thoroughly incorporate the oil and herb mixture with the potatoes making sure all of the pieces are completely coated (your hands work best here) and then spread the potatoes in a single layer throughout the pan. 4. Roast until potatoes are brown on the outside and soft on the inside—about 90 minutes. Occasionally scrape the bottom of the roasting pan with a spatula and turn the potatoes to brown them evenly and keep them from sticking to the pan. YIELDS ABOUT 4–6 SERVINGS

Garlic Smashed Potatoes

These have become a standard on many restaurant menus because of their slightly chewy texture which is a change from the standard issue mashed potatoes that don't require any teeth at all to eat!

The old fashioned potato masher works OK for small recipe batches like this. For larger batches of mashed potatoes and for those who insist on extra smooth potatoes, an electric hand mixer is the way to go. To strive for perfection in getting that extra smooth consistency, some chefs use a food mill or even a potato ricer which is essentially like a garlic press but large enough to accommodate potatoes. But that is messier than it all needs to be. The amount of garlic used comes down to personal preference. I suggest trying the amount recommended in the recipe and then the following times you make this, feel free to adjust the amount up or down according to your tastes. It is essential that the garlic be minced as finely as possible to avoid chewing into chunks of garlic! A garlic press is the ideal tool to accomplish this.

Good gravy! These smashed potatoes are tasty and moist enough on their own so they really don't need gravy to enjoy them. So to keep things simple, I originally left it out of this section. But for many, mashed potatoes and gravy are an inseparable combination. And even for those who don't feel this way, it's often the meat next to the mashed potatoes on the plate that really needs the gravy. So I have to address this need.

If convenience and simplicity are the top priorities, there are commercially made gravies available in a jar or those mixed from a packet of dry ingredients. These suffice for many families on a regular basis.

But for those who want something more special, there are already recipes in this book that can easily be adapted into really good gravies as long as you have some leftover meat drippings to work with. The *jus* that is part of the Roast Prime Rib au Jus is little more than beef gravy without flour to thicken it. To make this a beef gravy, whisk in just enough flour into the shallot and fat mixture after the shallots have softened to make a thin paste—that's a roux. (For flour thickened gravy, onions are OK instead of shallots.) Proceed with the rest of the recipe whisking in the liquid ingredients. Once the liquid comes to a simmer, the flour will start to thicken it. Looking at Sautéed Pork Medallions in a Pan Sauce, the pan sauce can be converted to gravy for poultry (preferably starting with fat drippings from poultry) by just whisking in flour as in the beef gravy but omitting the butter pieces, lemon juice, and parsley at the end.

Ingredients	*Procedure*
• 1 pound medium sized red potatoes (about 5) • Handful of kosher salt	1. Scrub and quarter the potatoes leaving the peels on. Some of the larger potatoes may need to be cut into smaller pieces so that all of the pieces are about the same size. 2. Place in a medium sized saucepan and cover with cold water to about 1 inch over the tops of the potatoes and add a handful of kosher salt to the water. Heat and bring to a boil; then turn down to a fast simmer. Cover and cook the potatoes just until they can be easily penetrated with a tip of a knife. First check in about 15 minutes. Do not overcook or the potatoes will become waterlogged.
• 4 cloves garlic, minced • ¼ cup half-and-half plus additional later if desired	3. While the potatoes are cooking, place the minced garlic with the half-and-half in another saucepan or a microwave proof container and heat the half-and-half until it just starts to come to a boil. Be extra careful not to let the half-and-half boil over!

Ingredients	*Procedure*
• ½ stick unsalted butter, softened • Kosher salt and freshly ground black pepper to taste	4. Using a colander, drain the potatoes and water into the sink and return the drained potatoes to saucepan used to cook the potatoes. Over medium low heat to quickly cook off any leftover water in the potatoes, break up the potatoes with a potato masher, adding the butter and then more half-and-half to get the desired moist and chunky consistency. Stir the contents thoroughly and remove to a serving dish. Serve immediately. SERVES 2–3

A few more words...

• For those who prefer the standard smooth mashed potatoes, peel the potatoes first before chopping up and simmering. Any kind of potato is suitable for mashing if the skins are not part of the dish; it doesn't have to be a red potato.

• Also please note that the garlic is always cooked briefly in some liquid to temper the harshness of raw garlic.

Sautéed Broccoli, Italian Style

My children didn't really like vegetables any more than most other children. But after I made this tasty dish for them the first time, they have regularly requested either this or sautéed spinach made the same way.

Using frozen vegetables eliminates the step of having to blanch the vegetables (briefly boiling them in water to soften them) before heating them in the oil. If **using frozen spinach instead of broccoli, be sure to squeeze the water out of the defrosted spinach over the sink before adding it to the oil.**

Ingredients	*Procedure*
• 10 oz. package frozen broccoli	1. Open the package and microwave on high power for about a minute or until the broccoli has been defrosted; set aside
• 3 tablespoons extra virgin olive oil	2. Heat a sauté pan over medium high heat and add the oil.
• 2 cloves garlic, minced (or substitute 2 teaspoons garlic powder)	3. Stir in the garlic, red pepper flakes, salt and pepper and heat until the garlic starts to give off an odor.
• Pinch of red pepper flakes	4. Before the garlic has a chance to burn, stir in the broccoli making sure that it is evenly coated with the oil/garlic mixture.
• Kosher salt and freshly ground black pepper to taste	5. Cover and turn down to medium heat allowing the broccoli to heat through and start to soften, about 3–4 minutes. Remove the cover and continue to cook another 1–2 minutes or until the water is cooked off and the broccoli starts to turn a very light shade of brown on the edges.
	SERVES 2–3

Creamed Spinach

This rich side dish is probably best known as a mainstay on steakhouse menus. Although some recipes simply sauté spinach in cream, the version I like uses a roux (flour and butter cooked together) thickened milk sauce known as a béchamel sauce as its foundation. Béchamel sauce is the foundation of many popular dishes like macaroni and cheese and that yummy sawmill gravy served on chicken fried steak. In fact, just about all of the gravies you can think of are just roux thickened liquids. I think you will find this section to be an especially instructive part of your cooking education.

To try and make the recipe especially clear, I have broken down the recipe into its two main components, the sautéed spinach and the béchamel sauce with added cheese. Once both are ready, they are combined and the dish is finished.

A couple of flavor contributors deserve mentioning here. It is possible to make a béchamel sauce just with the roux and milk. But while melting the butter to make the roux, why not add some chopped onions to boost the flavor? This is what often makes good professionally prepared food better than what the home cook makes. For example, while the home cook might be content with using water as an ingredient, the professional will use that opportunity to substitute something like broth or maybe fruit juice as appropriate to boost the flavor.

The other ingredient worth mentioning here is the nutmeg. Just like basil is really good with tomatoes, nutmeg is especially good with spinach and is a classic component of béchamel sauce although many of us have only tasted nutmeg as a seasoning in pumpkin pie or perhaps eggnog. Adding the right amount of nutmeg really elevates this dish to something special. But two things must be remembered: 1. Only buy whole nutmeg (now widely available in supermarkets) and grate it at the moment it is needed. The finest holes on a cheese grater will do just fine. and 2. Don't overdo it! A little bit of nutmeg goes a long way. Too much will overpower the dish. I start out conservatively with ½ teaspoon but after adding this, taste to see if you can detect the nutmeg. If not, keep adding small amounts until you can. When the finished dish has an interesting additional flavor and you can't quite figure out what it is, you've got it!

Ingredients	Procedure
Sautéed spinach • 1 stick butter, salted • 2 packages of frozen chopped spinach	1. Using medium low heat, melt 1 stick of the butter in a large sauté pan. Do not allow the butter to brown. 2. Defrost the spinach (the microwave oven is quickest). Squeeze out most of the water and then sauté over medium high heat in the sauté pan for a few minutes until the remaining water has been evaporated. Set the spinach aside, keeping it warm on low heat.
Béchamel sauce with cheese • ½ stick butter, salted • 1½ cups onion, finely chopped • ¼ cup all-purpose flour • 2 cups of milk • ½ teaspoon freshly grated nutmeg • ¼ pound of Monterey Jack cheese, shredded • Salt, pepper, and additional freshly grated nutmeg to taste	3. Meanwhile, over at the large saucepan, melt ½ stick of butter; add the chopped onions and turn the heat up to medium, sautéing the onions until soft—about 5 minutes. 4. In the meantime, scald the milk by placing it in a microwave-safe container and microwaving it on the high setting for about 4 minutes or until it just begins to bubble. Be extra careful not to let the milk boil over! 5. Using a whisk, blend the flour into the onion and butter mixture to begin making a roux. Continue whisking to avoid burning the mixture. As soon as the mixture has become a dry paste, gradually add the scalded milk, stirring with the whisk until a thick, bubbling, white sauce has been obtained. Add the nutmeg. Add the Monterey Jack cheese, stirring with the whisk until the cheese is melted and completely blended into the mixture.

Ingredients	Procedure
	6. Finally, add the reserved sautéed spinach into the white sauce mixture, gently stirring with the whisk until the spinach is thoroughly blended into the white sauce. Season, adding salt, pepper, and additional freshly grated nutmeg to taste. MAKES ABOUT 3 CUPS

A few more words...

Q. What is a sauce?

A. In general, a sauce is a flavorful liquid that is thickened to help it adhere to food.

OK, there are a number of 'sauces' like Worcestershire sauce that isn't really thickened but the above definition will give you a good working overview.

There are dozens of different sauces in this world with different names but most can be classified by:

1. The base liquid
2. The thickener
3. Any added ingredients (if any) that change the character of the sauce.

For example, the sauce in our creamed spinach starts with 1. milk and 2. is thickened by a roux to become a béchamel and 3. becomes a type of cheese sauce by the addition of the Monterey Jack.

Another example: 1. Liquefied tomatoes 2. thickened by evaporating some of the water out becomes tomato sauce.

Depending on the sauce, the base liquid can be milk, beef broth, chicken broth, tomatoes, etc. The thickener can be roux (flour mixed in fat to keep the flour from forming lumps) or corn starch among other possibilities. The clear sauces seen in Chinese restaurants are usually thickened with corn starch. The gravies we use over mashed potatoes and various meats are broths that are thickened with starch that is part of the flour in the roux. Because flour has protein in addition to starch, gravies made with it come out opaque instead of clear which is good. Most people would be turned off by see-through gravy on our meats and mashed potatoes! And as the tomato sauce example above shows, simple reduction by cooking off excess liquid can sometimes take the place of adding starch for thickening.

The category of sauces that doesn't quite fit in with all of this is the one that combines egg yolks and fat. When mechanically mixed with each other (along with other flavorful liquids), these form thick luxurious sauces. Egg yolks, oil, and lemon juice combined together make mayonnaise. Egg yolks, melted butter and lemon juice make hollandaise sauce. Change the lemon juice in hollandaise to white wine vinegar and add tarragon and you've got a béarnaise sauce.

The base liquid and thickener usually define a handful of 'mother' sauces.

A simplified list of roux based 'mother' sauces includes:

- milk + roux = white sauce (a.k.a. béchamel sauce)
- chicken broth + roux = velouté sauce
- beef broth + roux = brown sauce (a.k.a. espagñole sauce)

The experienced cook will likely recognize these as close relatives to the various gravies mentioned at the introduction for the Creamed Spinach dish. The different added ingredients define all of the dozens of derivative sauces that can result. Charts listing all of these sauces are a part of any professional cooking textbook. *For those wishing to learn more on this subject, see Sauces—A Family Tree in the Appendix.* Mastering sauce making on the professional level is a formidable undertaking. But for you, my intention in this little essay is to (hopefully) convey to you that the basic fundamentals of sauces aren't all that complicated.

When starting with a 'mother' sauce, another important derivative can be obtained by adding a liquid (milk and/or chicken broth) to give the dish the consistency of soup. Add the vegetable of your choice (e.g. mushrooms) and you have Cream of Mushroom Soup, our next recipe.

Cream of Mushroom Soup

"Mother' sauces also have a relationship to many cream soups. The difference between a velouté sauce and a cream soup is little more little more than adding either chicken broth as in this soup or perhaps clam broth if you are making a clam chowder and finishing with a milk product. When viewed in the right way, none of these dishes are very complicated, are they?

Looking at the recipe below, we have the mushrooms (dried and fresh) which will be cooked in the chicken broth. Then the roux is added and only then do we finish with the dairy products (half-and-half and heavy cream). The order is important because we want to expose the dairy products to only enough heat to bring the soup up to serving temperature and not curdle it.

Let's talk about some of the ingredients. Chicken broth is used as the base fluid to get this to a soup consistency instead of a sauce. But why chicken broth instead of say, water? It is because chicken broth contributes more flavor and body to the soup than just plain water. But interestingly enough, because of the predominance of the other ingredients, the soup doesn't taste like chicken! It just tastes richer than if it was made from just water. Canned chicken broth is more than adequate for this dish. Just try to buy a reduced sodium version to make sure that the amount of salt added to this dish doesn't get out of control. For those who wish to leave out meat products from this dish, a vegetable broth or even water will be good enough to get by.

The dried mushrooms supercharge the mushroom flavor when they are soaked in warm water and added to the soup. The most well known dried mushrooms are the Italian *porcini* mushrooms. These are indeed excellent but can be quite expensive, sometimes costing as much as $50 per pound! Fortunately, a little of this dried product goes a long way. Dried mushrooms other than the *porcini* coming from other parts of the world are a bit more reasonably priced and arguably, just as good.

Ingredients	*Procedure*
• ½ ounce dried mushrooms • ¾ cup warm water • 2–15 oz. cans reduced sodium chicken broth	1. Soak the dried mushrooms in the warm water for about 1 hour. Drain the water into a stockpot. (If there is an objectionably large amount of sediment left in the mushroom soaking water, pour it through a coffee filter.) Add the chicken broth to the stockpot and bring to a simmer.
• 2 tablespoons vegetable oil	2. Chop the soaked mushrooms into fairly fine pieces and sauté in the oil for about 5 minutes. Add these mushrooms to the chicken broth and then bring the broth mixture to a slow boil.
• ½ pound white mushrooms, sliced • 1 tablespoon butter, salted	3. Add butter to the sauté pan and sauté the white mushrooms over medium heat. When they are tender but not discolored (do not overcook), remove them from the pan and set aside.
• 2 tablespoons butter • 1 medium onion, diced very finely • 2 tablespoons flour	4. Sauté the onions in the butter over medium heat until they turn translucent but do not brown. Prepare a roux by sprinkling in the flour and stirring together for about 3 minutes until a paste-like consistency is obtained.

Ingredients	Procedure
• 1 cup half-and-half • ½ cup heavy cream • 1 teaspoon dried tarragon (optional) • Salt and pepper to taste	5. Add the roux mixture to the chicken broth and mix well with a whisk until the mixture is slightly thickened and any lumps are broken up. Add the sautéed white mushrooms and lower to a simmer for 10 minutes. Remove from the heat. Warm the half-and-half/heavy cream mixture to a simmer and then stir in along with the optional tarragon, salt and pepper if desired. Serve immediately. SERVES 5 TO 6.

Note: If the soup must be reheated, reheat very gently not allowing it to boil and possibly curdle.

A few more words...

Q. What can we do to prevent curdling?
A. Whenever dairy products are mixed with heat, there is the possibility of curdling which leaves the finished dish pretty unappetizing looking and tasting not quite as intended. The only way to try and prevent anything is to know what causes it.

There are three conditions that encourage curdling, any combination of which can apply to a certain dish.

1. Heat is the obvious first condition. In general, the higher the heat used the more likely curdling will happen when dairy products are included.

2. The less fat in the dairy product added to heat, the more chance of curdling. Heavy cream almost never curdles even when boiling it but milk is more likely to curdle. This is why sauce recipes with heavy cream often discourage substitutions with lighter fat products. Cream soups can pose more of a

problem because the milk fat is added to a large amount of other liquid which effectively makes it a lower fat product. The saving grace is that the starch that is part of the roux helps to create more stability and less chance for curdling.

3. Acid greatly encourages curdling. If the soup contains acid ingredients like tomatoes, curdling is more likely. Although sour cream is fairly high in fat, it curdles easily in the presence of heat because of its acid content that gives it its characteristic flavor. And because of its lower fat, yogurt is even worse in this regard. The best practical advice is that when adding sour cream or yogurt to finish a hot dish, take it off the heat and let it cool down to about serving temperature. Then stir in the dairy product and serve right away. As in the soup, if it must be reheated do it gently and do not allow it to boil after the dairy product has been added.

Crazy people? With all of this concern about preventing curdling, there are people who regularly heat milk and add acid to it just to make sure it curdles. Who are these crazy people? They are called *cheese makers*! After purposely making the milk curdle, they collect all the solid clumps, the *curds* and separate them from the liquid, the *whey*. Add a little salt, some aging time and perhaps some mold (not to mention a lot of know how) and cheese happens! Doing this same curdling process to soy milk gives us *tofu*.

Caesar Salad with Croutons

Here is a special salad often associated with fancy restaurants but if you can get a hold of some pasteurized eggs now becoming available in some supermarkets, you can effortlessly make this special treat in your own home without the worry of salmonella poisoning. And for those of you who want to go the extra mile and make your own croutons instead of using the pre-made ones in a box, I'll show you how. However, these croutons taste so good, you might want to eat them all before you have a chance to put them in the salad. Don't say I didn't warn you!

By now, many of you know about Caesar Cardini, a restaurateur in Tijuana who as the story goes, came up with this creation to satisfy a group of Hollywood stars who dropped in to his place after a night of partying in the 1920s. While we are not sure how true this story is, there is no disputing the widespread popularity of this salad in restaurants everywhere. There are even some upscale restaurants that make this in an elaborate tableside presentation. This, along with the classic recipe instructions that call for either a raw or partially cooked egg in the dressing, has likely discouraged many home cooks from trying this recipe. But with pasteurized in-shell eggs now available in many supermarkets, cooking of the eggs is no longer even necessary. I now use 2 egg yolks in place of the single whole egg in the original recipe to provide extra richness in the dressing.

This brings me to another point. Most classic recipes have evolved over the years to suit modern tastes and dietary practices. For example, I consider the anchovy paste to be indispensable but acknowledge that the original recipe did not include anchovies (other than being an ingredient of the Worcestershire sauce).

Because this is a minimalist recipe that gathers a small group of ingredients together without even cooking them, the quality of those ingredients is especially crucial to the success of the dish.

Ingredients	*Procedure*
• 2 hearts of romaine (or regular romaine heads of lettuce with the large outer leaves and tough stems removed)	1. Wash and dry before tearing into fork sized pieces.

Ingredients	*Procedure*
• 2 egg yolks (preferably from pasteurized eggs for safety against salmonella) • ⅓ cup extra virgin olive oil	2. Using a mixing bowl, whisk the egg yolks until smooth. Drizzle in the olive oil while continuously whisking to form a mayonnaise.
• 2 tablespoons freshly squeezed lemon juice (not bottled) • 1 teaspoon Worcestershire sauce • 1 small garlic clove, minced • ½ teaspoon anchovy paste (optional but highly recommended) • Salt, freshly ground black pepper, and/or additional lemon juice to taste	3. Whisk in the remaining ingredients. Taste and adjust seasonings to taste. Pour the over the romaine leaves and mix well.
• ½ cup freshly grated Parmigiano-Reggiano cheese	4. Sprinkle in the grated cheese and mix through but not quite enough to have all of the cheese disappear into the dressing.

Serve immediately with croutons on top (the recipe follows for some great homemade ones). SERVES 3–4

Croutons

Ingredients	*Procedure*
• 1 clove garlic, minced • 1 teaspoon dried basil • 1 teaspoon dried oregano • ½ teaspoon salt • ⅓ cup extra virgin olive oil	1. Thoroughly mix the garlic, basil, oregano, and salt into the olive oil with a whisk.
• ½ stick salted butter • 4 cups of ½ inch bread cubes (preferably made from Italian or French bread)	2. (If the 4 cups of bread cubes is too much for your sauté pan at one time, do this step in a couple of batches.) Heat a large sauté pan on medium high heat and add the butter and the olive oil mixture. When the butter is melted and mixed into the olive oil mixture, add the bread cubes, mixing well to make sure all of the cubes are coated evenly. Toss the cubes occasionally as they brown and remove them when they begin to lightly brown on all sides. 3. Cool and store in an airtight zipper bag or other container at room temperature until ready for use. If necessary, the croutons will keep for 3 to 4 days at room temperature. They should not be refrigerated.

A few more words...

Although olive oil has been with us going back to the ancient Greeks, there are many people who know little about this wonderful food. Besides its taste, it is now also popular because of the discovery that its mostly monounsaturated fat profile can improve our good (HDL) cholesterol/bad (LDL) ratio which is heart healthy. In addition, the Mediterranean Diet uses olive oil as its main source of fat to try and emulate those in that region of Europe who have lower rates of heart disease. But since dietary wisdom is constantly changing, let's just stick to how to shop for the best tasting olive oil.

Growing up, the taste of green olives was far from one of my favorites. But when I tasted my first extra virgin olive oil on a piece of crusty bread with a little salt and pepper, it was love at first bite! Even today, I don't care much for the taste of green olives. How could this be, I wondered? Later, I learned that in the making of olive oil, the juice which provides the bitterness of the olive is removed.

Most vegetable oils are refined in a factory where the oil is extracted by mechanical pressing, heat, and solvents. All oils treated this way including olive oil will have an <u>almost tasteless flavor profile</u>. Olive oils labeled as '**light**', '**extra-light**', and '**pomace**' fall into this category.

Extra virgin olive oil is entirely different since it is an unrefined oil—its essence is extracted from the first cold pressing <u>which preserves all of its rich olive flavor</u>. In addition, European standards require the oil to have an acid content below a certain level (less than 0.8%) to qualify as extra virgin. Oils that exceed this level usually land up being refined into one of the tasteless oils described above.

The result of the technical standards is that just about all extra virgin olive oil while not tasting exactly alike, is of a uniformly high quality. What is sometimes referred to as a supermarket extra virgin olive oil is sold by large companies such as Bertolli, Colavita and many others. The taste differences between brands is pretty subtle and often it is worthwhile to shop by price for larger sizes like 3 liter bottles or metal tins since the small sizes sold in stores can be outrageously expensive in comparison by the ounce. Olive oil that is kept in a sealed container away from heat and light (but not refrigerated) should last for about a year without going rancid.

Also being marketed is an artisan type of extra virgin olive oil sold in specialty food stores produced in small batches from individual groves of olive trees—just like the way some vintage wines are marketed. I will leave it to those with the inclination and the pocketbook to try these and come up with their own opinions on whether these expensive products are worth the money.

Finally, there is a hybrid product that is commonly marketed as '**pure olive oil**'. It is simply tasteless refined olive oil that is enhanced by some extra virgin olive oil to give it some flavor. Its main attraction is that it costs a little less than extra virgin oil and may appeal to those who like the taste of olive oil but find the extra virgin oil a bit overpowering in flavor.

When using a flavorful olive oil like extra virgin or pure, the most flavor benefit comes from its being in the raw state. Extra virgin even has some flavor benefit in low temperature pan frying of something like chicken Parmesan (if you buy it in a large enough quantity to make it affordable) but it will burn easily if used for high temperature sautéing.

Appendix

By now you have noticed that along with the recipes, I have tried to impart some basic knowledge to add to your education on food and cooking. For some, this will be enough but others are more inquisitive and will want to learn a little more beyond the basics. For those more inquisitive folks I have added some additional material that hopefully will be of interest to you without cluttering up the body of the cookbook with material that may not be of general interest to everybody.

This book has served as your training wheels to get you started on the journey to discover the wonderful world of food and cooking. Hopefully armed with a newly found appreciation of the subject, you will check out the Recommended Reading and Watching section to continue your journey of discovery. Perhaps some of you will be inspired to enter the cooking field as a professional. Even if you are just cooking for friends or your family, they will sense the love you put into your cooking. And doesn't that alone make it all worthwhile?

It has been a privilege to be able to share some of what I have learned from others through the years about food and cooking by way of this book. I sincerely hope that you receive the same satisfaction in learning from this book that I have gotten from writing it.

Beef—A Geographic Tour

More fat <<<<<<<<——————————————>>>>>>>>>>>More lean

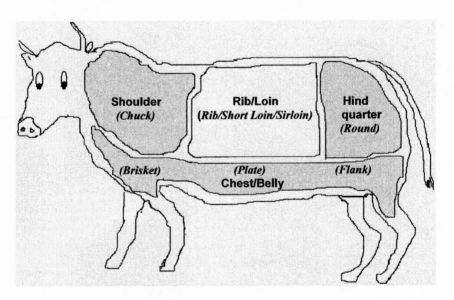

- Primal cuts are in *(Italics)*
- The areas shown in Gray support most of the animal's weight and are therefore, not naturally tender.

Let's examine each area in a little more detail:

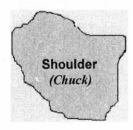

The *Chuck* area is fatty and tough which means that although it requires slow cooking methods to tenderize it, the fat along with its abundant connective tissue that is converted into gelatin will help to keep it moist. This makes it an ideal choice for a stew or pot roast. Ground chuck has about 20% fat and makes the tastiest and juiciest ground beef for burgers.

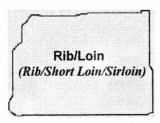

Rib/Loin
(Rib/Short Loin/Sirloin)

The *Rib* section is next to the Chuck and along with being very tender is more fatty which makes for a very juicy cut of beef. The rib-eye steak (sometimes known as a Delmonico steak) is a favorite of many. The rib roast (sometimes called Prime Rib even if it is not USDA Prime graded beef) is the best beef roast available for flavor, tenderness, and juiciness.

The *Short Loin* is the home of the T-bone and Porterhouse steaks, the Porterhouse having the larger filet section (a part of the tenderloin muscle).

The tenderloin is the tenderest part of the animal since it receives the least amount of exercise and commands the highest prices. It is often sold separately as filet mignon and commands the highest prices of all the beef cuts because of this tenderness. But because it is very lean, it has a somewhat milder beef flavor than other cuts and often needs help from bacon strips or sauces to boost its flavor and moisture.

When the filet section is sold separately, the remaining outside part of the steak is called a Strip Steak. It is not quite as tender and juicy as a rib steak but has a wonderful beefy chewiness and flavor that makes it a great steak in its own right.

The *Sirloin* is essentially a transition section to the tougher Round at the rear of the animal. It is not quite as tender as the Short Loin section and is a bit leaner since it is toward the rear of the animal. However, sirloin can be surprisingly good and is normally priced a lot cheaper than the other loin and rib cuts giving it perhaps the best bang for the buck among tender cuts of beef. Ground sirloin is a good alternative for those who prefer a less fatty alternative to ground chuck.

Hind quarter
(Round)

The *Round* section is the most difficult to handle from a cooking standpoint because it is both a tough piece of meat and a lean one. Long, slow cooking to make it tender can have a tendency to dry it out because there is so little internal fat to provide moisture. The two main ways to deal with this kind of cut are:

• Slow cook it to make it tender but provide plenty of cooking liquid and/ or gravy to make the meat moist enough to be palatable. Because the round can be cut into large flat steaks, it lends itself to being pounded thinly and made into stuffed rolled steaks for braising called *roulades* or its Italian name, *braciole*.

- Roast it like a more tender cut of beef, being careful not to overcook it but then slice it very thinly to make it tender to the palate.

Ground round is the choice for those who want ground beef with the least amount of fat. But it is relatively dry and flavorless for most tastes.

The chest and belly of four legged animals are some of the hardest working muscles and thus the toughest parts. But with the proper cooking and slicing techniques, these cuts can make surprisingly good eating.

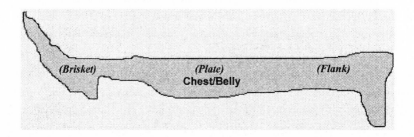

The *Brisket* which is the chest muscle of the steer is one of the toughest of all cuts of meat. But because it has plenty of fat, it can withstand long slow cooking to tenderize it without drying it out. The main methods are to slow cook it in liquid until the meat becomes tender or slow cook it over a low smoky fire—a favorite in Texas style barbeque. In addition, cured meat products like corned beef and pastrami often come from the brisket.

The *Plate* is a rather obscure primal cut but it is the home of what is called short ribs, known as a tough cut that has to be slow cooked in liquid to be tender enough to eat. But its ample fat makes it quite tasty. Japanese and Koreans enjoy this cut quickly grilled over high heat when cut about ¼ inch thick across the grain of the meat and bones (known by butchers as a *flanken* cut).

The *Flank* steak had for a long time been ignored as a tough cheaper cut of meat, suitable only for slow cooking in liquid since the stringy abdominal muscles were apparently too lean to cook over dry heat. Since then, it has been discovered that if this steak is first marinated to give it some flavor and moisture, grilled to no more than medium rare, and then sliced thinly across the grain making the stringy muscles into short tender segments—this becomes a flavor powerhouse sometimes known as London broil. Just to confuse things, some supermarkets will also label roasts coming from the sirloin or round as London broil but I feel this method works best with flank steak. Another less commonly marketed cut of meat that also responds well to this treatment is *skirt steak* which comes from the diaphragm of the animal, a muscle wall that separates the chest and abdominal cavities. It is now popularly used for the Mexican classic, beef *fajitas.*

Pork—A Geographic Tour

More fat <<<<<<<<———————————————>>>>>>>>>>>More lean

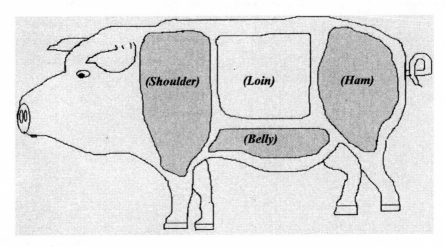

- Primal cuts are in *(Italics)*
- The areas shown in Gray support most of the animal's weight and are therefore, not as naturally tender.

The *Shoulder* because it has ample fat through it makes it great for slow cooking until it becomes fall-off-the-bone tender. Pulled pork is simply this cut that has been slow cooked over smoke (barbecued) until it can be literally pulled off the bone and shredded for sandwiches. A roast that is called *Pork Butt* or sometimes *Boston Butt* is actually part of the shoulder, not the rear end as the word 'butt' would lead you to believe. And also because of this ample fat, the shoulder is the primary choice for various pork sausages.

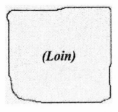

Instead of giving separate primal names to the rib and loin like for beef, the whole area is designated as the *Loin* for primal cut purposes. It includes the pork chops in the rib section which look like a smaller version of a beef rib steak and those in the loin section which look like a miniature T-bone steak. Because these are from the most tender part of the animal, they respond best to high heat cooking just like for beef steak, either in a sauté pan or on the grill.

But the loin is not always sold as complete pork chops. Sometime the meat is sold separate from the bones in the form of *boneless pork loin* or *pork tenderloins*. The leftover rib bones from the loin section are sold sometimes for more than the meat due to the popularity of *baby back ribs*, especially in restaurants. Because this rib meat comes from a tender part of the animal, it takes very little time or skill to yield a tender finished product. But because of its high price along with the considerable amount of bone involved, it gives the worst bang for the buck in the way of edible meat. *Spare ribs* from the belly part of the animal are discussed later.

What is sold in stores as *country style ribs* come from the transitional area between the loin and shoulder, those from closer to the loin being leaner. *Sirloin chops* are from the transitional area between the loin and ham. The *center cut loin* which includes the pork chops but doesn't include these transitional portions is considered to be the most desirable.

Because the loin is a much leaner cut of meat than the shoulder it is therefore easier to overcook and dry out. We have all eaten pork chops that were as tough as shoe leather. This is because of cooking guidelines in the past that required all pork to be cooked to well done to avoid the possibility of illness from any possible trichinosis. But with today's pork being bred for much leaner meat than in generations past, the well done pork chop is just too tough and dry for most palates. Fortunately, reason is starting to finally win out over fear. With today's modern pork producing practices, trichinosis is far less common than before. In addition, trichinosis is killed when the meat reaches an internal temperature of 137°F (medium rare) so cooking to a maximum internal temperature of between 150–155°F leaves the inside of the meat a faint pink color ensuring enough juiciness with an ample margin for safety against trichinosis.

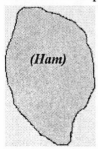

(Ham)

At the hind quarter of the animal is the ***ham***. Most of us associate ham as being pink colored and smoky tasting, as result of curing with sodium nitrate and smoking over hardwood. The Italian style ham, *prosciutto* is cured and dried but not smoked. This was all originally done as a way to help preserve the meat before refrigeration came along. Now, we mainly use this process because it tastes good but the uncured product known as *fresh ham* is also quite good when roasted and sliced thin. But since few of us buy ham in this form, it is not very commonly found in stores.

The *belly* of the pig is fatty and without as much meat as the top part of the animal so it would seem that there is little of interest there. But pork fat has such a sweet flavor that we can take the outside part of the belly, cure it and smoke it like ham and produce a food that has one of the world's great cooking aromas—*bacon*! Again, the Italians have their own style of bacon known as *pancetta* which is cured but not smoked. It is sold in Italian specialty stores and some supermarket delis rolled up to look like a jelly roll. It is a classic ingredient of spaghetti *carbonara*. What is known in the U.S. as *Canadian bacon* or in Canada, *back bacon* comes from the loin, not the belly.

Underneath the bacon on the belly side of the animal are the *spare ribs*. Although few parts of the pig can truly be called tough because we send them to market at a young age, the spare ribs simply cannot be cooked the same way a pork chop is cooked on the grill or they will be too tough to eat. They require either slow cooking in liquid or more commonly, slow cooking over smoke (barbecuing). Because of its ample fat, this cut takes quite well to this cooking method without drying out. Although restaurants tend to favor the baby back rib because it is tender to begin with and is thus easier to cook, most barbecue purists prefer the spare rib for its pleasantly chewy texture (after it is slow cooked long enough) and depth of flavor that baby backs cannot match. The *St. Louis style spare rib* has the top meaty part with the cartilage removed (which is sold in some markets as rib tips) for easier cooking and eating. The St. Louis style rib is becoming more popular in supermarkets and is well worth looking for despite its higher price compared to regular spare ribs. When it comes to shopping for spare ribs—size matters! Here, *smaller* is better. The larger the rack of ribs, the older the animal is that it came from and the tougher it is likely to be. Try to select the trimmed St. Louis style racks of spare ribs weighing about 2¼ pounds or less. If St. Louis style ribs are not available where you shop, the standard untrimmed spare rib will be available but try to select a rack under about 3½ pounds or you may land up with some tough eating no matter how you cook it.

Sauces—A Family Tree

Sauces are a more important part of our food than most people realize. Sure we all know about the sauce that goes on our pasta but so many other foods like gravies, the cheese part of macaroni and cheese, ketchup and even salad dressings are actually sauces. In case you missed it, check out the *A few more words...* section at the end of the Creamed Spinach recipe where I introduced this subject. To review, a sauce is generally a flavorful liquid that is thickened to help it adhere to food.

There are dozens of different sauces in this world with different names but most can be classified by:

1. The base liquid
2. The thickener
3. Any added ingredients (if any) that change the character of the sauce.

So the good news is that almost all of these sauces can be classified under a handful of thickened base liquids (1. and 2. above) which are the foundation of what we call *mother sauces* or sometimes *leading sauces*. The choice of added ingredients (3. above) determines the sauce's final identity.

Although we make a few elementary sauces as part of this cookbook, sauce making by chefs in upscale restaurants can get quite involved. To give you an idea of this, check out the professional teaching cookbooks listed in the next section. In fact, there are whole books dedicated to the subject, the most definitive probably being a near 600 page volume titled appropriately enough, *Sauces* by James Peterson, Wiley (1998).

So while a section in a basic cookbook cannot really cover this subject in any depth, I think the interested cook may find an overview of this subject to be worthwhile in getting a grasp of the big picture when it comes to cooking.

Some history... We do know a little about sauces from civilizations going back to ancient Greece and Rome. Until the French began to refine sauce making a few centuries ago, most sauces had powerful flavorings that were used to make bland food more palatable or perhaps help hide the taste of foods that were past their prime. While modern refrigeration has helped deal with the second issue, we still use strong sauces to add interest to relatively bland foods. These are normally classified as *condiments* whereas a *sauce* as the French though of it was something to accompany the food's inherent flavors. This evolution by the French which simplified sauce making along with taking out some of the overkill in seasoning was first standardized early in the nineteenth century by Antonin Carême (1784–1833) and refined near the turn of the twentieth century by the publication of *Le Guide Culinaire* by another legendary French chef Georges Auguste Escoffier (1847–1935), a book still in use today. The simplified system of *mother sauces* we use today is one of their many contributions to the culinary field.

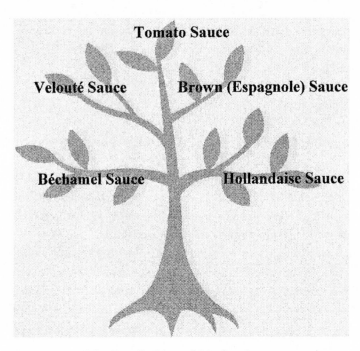

The Family Tree of *Mother Sauces*

This group of sauces is generally considered to represent the hot sauces (as opposed to cold sauces like mayonnaise) in use today. Here is a simplified outline chart describing each one proceeding clockwise around the tree:

Sauce	Liquid	Thickening Agent
Béchamel	Milk	Roux
Velouté	Chicken/Veal/Fish Stock	Roux
Tomato	Pureed or Crushed Tomatoes	Roux or Reduction
Brown (Espagnole)	Beef Stock	Roux
Hollandaise	Butter	Egg Yolks

As you can see, hollandaise not being a roux sauce is different from the others which is why some people who do these lists don't consider hollandaise as belonging to this list.

The other item worth noting above is the word 'stock' instead of the word 'broth' because many writers use the two interchangeably which might cause confusion the first time you see this in a book. Sorting out the difference between these terms really gets into hair-splitting and not everybody agrees on the definitions so let's just simplify things by saying that the word 'broth' is normally used by home cooks and the word 'stock' is usually used by restaurant cooks.

Now let's look at each of the mother sauces and some of the ones derived from them.

Béchamel Sauce is sometimes known as 'white sauce' or 'cream sauce' although it doesn't necessarily have cream in it. The thickness and richness that reminds one of cream is provided by the butter and flour in the roux. Although flavorings like onions and nutmeg are often used to add some flavor, béchamel is a very bland sauce that normally acts as a rich background to complement to other ingredients in a dish. The sawmill gravy that goes on either fried chicken or more often, chicken fried steak is a béchamel sauce. Béchamel sauce is also a topping for the famous Greek eggplant casserole dish, *moussaka* and sometimes appears in Italian dishes like *lasagna Bolognese* which uses a combination of tomato and béchamel sauces.

But usually béchamel sauce appears in dishes with other ingredients added, most notably cheese. The version of creamed spinach in the book recipe uses a béchamel sauce with a little Monterey Jack cheese for flavoring. Adding cheddar cheese to a béchamel is known as a *cheddar cheese sauce* that is also the foundation of most macaroni and cheese recipes.

Velouté Sauce is probably best known to the home cook as chicken gravy although it can be made from any white stock like veal or fish. Of course the choice of stock would depend on the food the sauce is supposed to be paired with.

Just like béchamel, velouté usually appears in dishes with other ingredients added but most notably cream which makes it into a *suprême sauce*. Add mushrooms to that and we have a mushroom sauce that is the basis for a tuna noodle casserole sauce that tastes a whole lot better than one made from canned cream of mushroom soup. And there is of course our own version of cream of mushroom soup in the recipes.

Tomato Sauce is classically made with a roux as a thickener but since the flour and butter tend to mute some of the tomato flavor, thickening by just simmering off the water (reduction), is the standard practice nowadays. But the version with the roux and some chicken stock is the basis for a tomato soup that is a whole lot better than what you can get from a can.

There are lots of derivatives of tomato sauce depending on the ingredients added and how much the sauce is reduced. When wine becomes part of the prominent flavors, you have the basis for the sauce in dishes like chicken *cacciatore*. And adding paprika and sour cream is the basis for the Hungarian classic, chicken *paprikash*. Adding a sweet and sour combination, usually molasses and vinegar gives you a tomato based *barbecue sauce*. When a tomato sauce is reduced to something thicker it is more intensely seasoned and is used in small amounts as a condiment. *Tomato ketchup* is just a thickened sweetened tomato sauce. Adding some horseradish to the ketchup leads to *cocktail sauce*, the favorite dip for shrimp cocktail. And *salsa* is just the Spanish word for sauce.

Brown or espagnole sauce is part of the technically most complicated family of roux thickened sauces. In its most basic form we have beef gravy. But since the derivative sauces are normally used to flavor very robust flavored meats, classic recipes call for a more concentrated form of this sauce to start with known as *demiglace* which in simplified terms is a brown sauce where the water is cooked out (reduced) to the point that it becomes a thin syrup. Because the derivative sauces are classically made from the demiglace and not brown sauce, demiglace is listed by some as one of the *mother sauces* instead of brown or espagnole sauce.

Many sauces can be derived from the demiglace; most all of them are expensive to make and their authentic versions are mostly only offered at elite restaurants with classically trained chefs. For some examples—adding reduced red wine gives us a *bordelaise sauce*, a great companion to a grilled flank steak. Madeira and port wines are powerful flavorings that are also used. And adding sour cream to a demiglace produces a great sauce for the Russian classic, beef *stroganoff*.

Hollandaise sauce is a different breed of cat from the roux based sauces. Butter and egg yolks are beaten together along with some lemon juice to form what is called an *emulsion* where different usually unmixable liquids are held together in suspension. Oil and vinegar mixed together to form a vinaigrette is an example of a temporary emulsion—once it is left alone long enough, it separates. Hollandaise is famous for being a finicky sauce to make and not have it separate. It is often used as a sauce for chicken, vegetables and fish—especially salmon. It is also an indispensable part of eggs *benedict*. Adding whipped cream makes it a *mousseline sauce*.

An important variation of hollandaise sauce is *béarnaise sauce*. Instead of the lemon juice as in hollandaise to provide the tart contrast to the rich butter and egg yolks, some reduced white wine vinegar is used along with tarragon, an herb with an anise-like flavor. While it can be used just about anywhere hollandaise is used, béarnaise is especially good on a steak.

Other sauces…

Mayonnaise is one of the most important sauces of all but since it is a cold sauce, it doesn't usually share top billing with the *mother sauces*. It has the most in common with hollandaise since they are both emulsions of egg yolks, lemon juice and fat (in this case oil instead of butter).

Traditional mayonnaise is made with a flavorless vegetable oil since it is usually meant to add some richness and moisture to other foods rather than a whole lot of flavor. The Provençal specialty from France called *aïoli*, ups the ante by using extra virgin olive oil and garlic along with the lemon juice—similar to the dressing for Caesar salad.

If you consider the many mayonnaise based salad dressings, there are many mayonnaise based sauces in addition to *tartar sauce* and *rémoulade sauce* which are often served with seafood.

Pasta sauce is so much more than tomato sauce considering that some of the most famous Italian sauces like *pesto sauce* were around long before tomatoes were introduced to the Old World.

Condiment sauces which don't fit into any of the Western attempts to categorize sauces include Worcestershire sauce, soy sauce, teriyaki sauce and the various fish sauces that are an important part of Thai and Vietnamese cooking.

Dessert sauces include crème anglaise, an egg yolk based sauce flavored with vanilla, caramel sauces, chocolate sauces and more.

We've just scratched the surface…I hope that this outline has given you a better appreciation of the world of sauces and interested you enough to explore this subject further on your own.

Recommended Reading and Watching

Just as some women like to collect shoes, I like to collect cookbooks. There are so many cookbooks competing for our attention that it's difficult to sort them all out. This is my list of books that are either noteworthy and/or have touched my life in some way. You will find that most of them are older books. This is not to say that the newer books aren't as good—far from it! It's just that as my book collection got larger, space became more limited and I got more stubborn about not buying more books to add to the collection unless it was something that was really an improvement over what I already had.

There are many ways to check out the books below or ones in general. Books can be previewed at bookstores or online at sites like www.amazon.com, www.bn.com, www.borders.com and others. The Amazon and Borders sites will often let you preview a few select pages of a book and read lots of reader reviews. All can give you information about buying books used that are out of print. Of course there is the good old-fashioned library. If you don't find the book you are looking for there, ask the librarian about interlibrary loans which will bring the book to your local library if you are willing to wait a week or two for it. And for those without computers, libraries often have computers with high speed Internet connections that you can use to research the above sites for books.

I have tried to classify these as best I could. Books that I refer to as 'teaching' cookbooks emphasize cooking theory and technique at least as much as the recipes.

All Purpose, General Interest Cookbook

The All New, All Purpose Joy of Cooking
by Marion Rombauer Becker, et al
- **Hardcover**: 1152 pages
- **Publisher**: Scribner; Revised edition (1997)

As a collector of mostly specialty cookbooks, all purpose cookbooks are not of particular interest to me. But for many cooks, at least one book of this type is a must for general recipe reference. A book that has been loved for generations, it was interesting when the publisher decided to totally overhaul it by farming it out to a committee of food experts in various fields. The result is a remarkable collection of recipes and food information although there are some purists who prefer the old version. I think the size of it can be overwhelming for the beginner which is a major reason I wrote this book whose size and contents are easier to grasp for the inexperienced cook to get his or her feet wet.

All Purpose, Teaching Cookbooks

The Cook's Bible: The Best of American Home Cooking
by Christopher Kimball
- **Hardcover:** 464 pages
- **Publisher:** Little, Brown; 1st ed edition (1996)

Christopher Kimball is the Editor and Founder of *Cook's Illustrated* magazine, a bimonthly publication dedicated to perfecting recipes for home cooking. This early effort of Kimball's is one of the best basic instructional cookbooks ever. Because *Cook's* doesn't accept advertising, the magazine and this book can write opinions about cookware and foods by brand name (even though some of the recommendations are now out of date.)

Master Recipes
by Stephen Schmidt
- **Hardcover:** 941 pages
- **Publisher:** Clear Light Books; 2nd edition (1998)

When I first started reading *Cook's Illustrated*, it was apparent to me that one of the contributors, Stephen Schmidt was a very talented cook and teacher. His 1987 book, *Master Recipes* was out of print but surely at least partly as a result of his contributions to *Cook's*, a number of people including myself bought copies from stores that offer out of print books. Eventually, the book came back into print. In addition, Schmidt was selected as one of the contributors to the *All New, All Purpose Joy of Cooking* described above. This book remains one of the best and most readable teaching cookbooks ever written.

James Beard's Theory & Practice of Good Cooking
by James Beard
- **Hardcover** : 465 pages
- **Publisher:** Knopf (1977)

Although a few of James Beard's books are still in print, the library is the best bet for finding his books. Just like in any good instructional book, Beard is wonderful at explaining food and cooking technique. Those who are interested in learning more about one of the all time greats in the culinary field should check out some of his writings.

Professional Teaching Cookbooks

The Professional Chef, Seventh Edition
by the Culinary Institute of America (Editor)
- **Hardcover**: 1056 pages
- **Publisher**: Wiley; 7th edition (2001)

Professional Cooking
by Wayne Gisslen
- **Hardcover**: 1120 pages
- **Publisher**: Wiley; 5th edition (2002)

These are the two main textbooks used in professional cooking classes. One is by the Culinary Institute of America (the other CIA), one of the most prestigious cooking schools in the world and the other is by a CIA graduate. When each new edition comes out, their respective publishers up the ante by adding more color illustrations and recipes. Both are superb books for those who want to learn just about everything worth learning about food and cooking but I prefer Gisslen's book because his more conversational writing style explains things a little better and is a little more reader friendly for me. In addition, his format of the individual recipe write-ups is a bit easier to follow—a format that I adopted for this book. Like all professional recipe books, they are written for quantity cooking. But even if you don't want to scale back the recipes for home cooking, the food and technique instruction by itself is worth it.

Food Science Teaching

Cookwise : The Secrets of Cooking Revealed
by Shirley Corriher

- **Hardcover:** 544 pages
- **Publisher:** Morrow Cookbooks; 1st edition (1997)

Shirley Corriher, who has a background as a research biochemist has been in demand as a food science consultant for among others, *Cook's Illustrated* and has made appearances on Food Network's *Good Eats*, a show hosted by Alton Brown on food science. So when she decided to write a book, people were interested. Although the recipe layouts are maddening to a lot of people, if you get this book to learn about food science, you will be glad you did. Once again, this is a case of somebody who has a good conversational writing style that explains things well.

On Food and Cooking: The Science and Lore of the Kitchen
by Harold McGee
- **Hardcover:** 896 pages
- **Publisher:** Scribner; Revised and Updated edition (2004)

The first edition of this book from 1984 has been a reference standard for serious cooks for some time now. But truth be known, unless you are a chemist who loves discussing carbon bonds, it can be a tough read after a while. The latest edition is greatly expanded and far more reader friendly for the non-scientist. While most of us will just want to jump in and read whatever subject interests us at the moment, this is the most comprehensive reference source for food science written for the lay person although it should be pointed out that **there are no recipes in this book**.

General Interest Cookbooks

The Simply Great Cookbook: Recipes and the Experience of Fine Dining from the Kitchens of Chuck Muer
by Chuck Muer
- **Paperback:** 166 pages
- **Publisher:** Momentum Books Limited (1992)

I wrote about finding this obscure book in my introduction to the Crab Cakes recipe. Despite having all of the wonderful seafood recipes, it is still a hard book to find. Your best chance is an online bookseller or the publisher at <u>www.momentumbooks.com</u>

Taste : One Palate's Journey Through the World's Greatest Dishes
by David Rosengarten
- **Paperback:** 352 pages
- **Publisher:** Random House (1998)

Back in the early 90s when visiting an out of town relative, I noticed a new cable channel called TV Food Network. All cooking shows all the time! This is living!! (Too bad it took years to make it onto my cable system back home.) Perhaps my favorite show at the time was *Taste* starring David Rosengarten. Unlike most other cooking shows then or now, he devoted the whole half hour show to one dish. What better opportunity to finally get a dish as close to perfection as possible? His book by the same name is a collection of classic dishes that undergoes his attempts at perfection. Admittedly, he can be a little too picky about some procedures and ingredients (even for me!) but the book is nonetheless enjoyable and very instructive reading. Recipes aside, his chapter at the end on pairing wines with foods is wonderfully informative.

Chef Paul Prudhomme's Seasoned America
by Paul Prudhomme
- **Hardcover:** 306 pages
- **Publisher:** Cookbooks; 1st ed edition (October, 1991)

Paul Prudhomme became one of America's favorite chefs through making spicy foods like blackened redfish famous outside of New Orleans. His treatment of American classics is no less interesting. Many of the dishes he tackles are old bland standards that he perks up by the use of spice mixtures. As one who hates bland food, this was a wake up call for me how important seasoning is to the success of a dish. And for those who want to learn more about Cajun-Creole cooking, his *Louisiana Cooking* is worthwhile reading, too.

The Complete Book of Pasta: An Italian Cookbook
by Jack Denton Scott
- **Paperback:** 333 pages
- **Publisher:** Bantam (1970)

This was an old paperback book I found gathering dust in the cellar of my mother's house. Since I was into any cookbook I could get my hands on, I took the book and studied it and cooked some dishes. The author was extremely opinionated and for one thing, did not believe in using tomato paste in a spaghetti sauce.

When I tasted the marinara sauce made out of Italian plum tomatoes and no paste, I knew I was on to something. And then there was the recipe for Bolognese sauce which he said was the classic one. And once again, I knew I was on to something. Although I have tweaked his Bolognese sauce recipe over the years and don't fuss with adding chicken livers like in his recipe, my culinary life was changed forever by this little paperback book. I do not believe it is in print any longer but like many older books like this, it can be found in libraries or for sale online as a used book.

The Frugal Gourmet
The Frugal Gourmet Cooks Three Ancient Cuisines: China, Greece, and Rome
The Frugal Gourmet on Our Immigrant Ancestors: Recipes You Should Have Gotten from Your Grandmother
by Jeff Smith
These are three out of a whole series of books written by Jeff Smith. Just about all are worthwhile reading with good recipes and can be found in many libraries. The last two are especially interesting for those who want to learn about international cuisine. My passion for cooking started after becoming hooked on TV cooking shows, especially *The Galloping Gourmet* (someone who was serious about food but not so serious about himself) and *The Frugal Gourmet* (someone who taught me to be serious about ingredients). Cooking satisfying dishes from the Frug's cookbooks led to a voracious appetite for studying other cookbooks until I decided to take some formal cooking classes to enhance my self taught knowledge. Unfortunately, his career was ended by a sexual abuse scandal in the late 90s that was settled out of court. He then lived in relative obscurity until his death in 2004. I just hope that he will eventually be remembered more for his worthwhile contributions to cooking than for the scandal; but human nature being what it is that seems doubtful.

Magazines

Magazines like *Gourmet* and *Bon Appetit* with all their pretty pictures and scenery are sexier than *Cook's Illustrated*. But they also have a lot of ads. If the pretty pictures and scenery are appealing to you, then these are pleasant magazines to read. But if you are mostly interested in the recipes, their website www.epicurious. com is a valuable resource for online recipes.

Cook's Ilustrated is all about trying to find the perfect recipe and the perfect ingredients and equipment to prepare it for the home cook. It is no-nonsense and has no ads. Although *Consumer Reports,* also available online at www.consumerreports. org does some fine articles reviewing food and cooking equipment, *Cook's* can review more of these products because this is their specialty. The magazine comes out once every other month. In addition, they have a growing collection of cookbooks covering many specialties. If you get hooked on this magazine as I did, you can order bound sets of back issues. Better yet, you can purchase an annual subscription to their website www.cooksillustrated.com and have access to all of the recipes and product reviews that have previously appeared in the magazine going back to the early 90s.

TV

Although some of the other cable channels have travel shows dealing with food, the only places that regularly feature cooking shows are PBS, usually on Saturdays and Food Network every day.

PBS is renowned for giving us Julia Child, Jeff Smith, Jacques Pépin, and many others too numerous to mention. They now offer *America's Test Kitchen* starring the gang from *Cook's Illustrated.* I have spent many a Saturday learning from PBS cooking shows over the years and I am grateful for that. But some of the PBS cooks have more recently adopted the practice of not giving out measurements for many of the recipes they demonstrate on the show. If you want those, you often have to buy their book. That amounts to a program that is little more than an infomercial for the book—and on top of that, the show is being supported with donations at least in part by 'viewers like you'. I think there is something wrong with this picture.

On the other hand, Food Network shows come with commercials but you can always get the complete recipes from all of their shows for free from their website www.foodnetwork.com In addition, their site maintains a large database of recipes and has other resources like instructional videos. Unless you have digital cable or satellite TV with an on screen program listing, the easiest way to get the daily schedule is from the website if you have a computer with an online connection.

There are a large number of different shows for different tastes but two of the most instructive shows on the basics are *Food 911* starring Tyler Florence who presents a wide variety of menus and great instruction to suit the needs of home cooks he visits and cooks with on each show and *Good Eats* starring Alton Brown which bests satisfies my hunger to learn more about the science and even the history behind food but with an entertaining flair. In addition, 'AB' has also been busy publishing some books like *I'm Here for the Food* and *Alton Brown's Gear for Your Kitchen* which are well worth a look at your bookstore or library. However, you may get the impression especially after reading the second book that you *need* all the kitchen equipment he lists in the book. And for the less experienced cook, that just isn't so!

Recipe Credits

Is there really such a thing as a truly original recipe? Even the most creative new dishes are almost always refinements of existing recipes. Because this book deals with established classic dishes that have been around and been refined for some time, my task was to determine which refinements for each dish lead to the best combination of great taste and ease of preparation. Both are important—no matter how great a dish might taste, if it is too difficult for the reader to make, it won't make it into the cook's repertoire.

Many times I laid out as many as 4 or 5 recipes for the same dish side by side, comparing and combining ideas and ingredient combinations. Sometimes a resulting composite recipe happens that is an improvement on all of the others. Other times I have gotten good results from refining and adapting one particularly good recipe. In the spirit of recognizing the efforts of others, those recipe sources are listed below.

But just because a book has recipes developed by others doesn't make it a bad thing as long as credit is properly given. Each of the classic dishes can have countless recipe versions developed over the years. Which one of those versions gives us that ideal combination of great taste and ease of preparation? It takes a lot of time, experience, and experimentation to come up with answers. In relying on a book like this, you are allowing the author to do the investigation for you, hopefully with results you will find worthwhile enough to become a part of your cooking repertoire.

Pasta with Tomato Sauce and Meatballs

This is a dish I first learned to make from my mother. But as mentioned in the Recommended Reading, *The Complete Book of Pasta: An Italian Cookbook* by Jack Denton Scott, Bantam (1970) was instrumental in perfecting my tomato sauce recipe over the years.

Chili con Carne

This recipe was adapted from "Passion Chili", a recipe from *Mike Kalina's Pittsburgh Cookbook* by Mike Kalina, Pina Books (1991). Kalina, who was the restaurant critic for the *Pittsburgh Post-Gazette* got the recipe from Kevin Cogan, an Indy race car driver who demonstrated it on a local Pittsburgh TV show.

Jambalaya, Creole-Style
Adapted from Earl Peyroux's recipe demonstrated on his long running PBS series from the 90s, *Gourmet Cooking*. Both he and his show were simple and unpretentious but very instructive—qualities that would be unlikely to land him a cooking show today on cable TV.

Roast Prime Rib of Beef au Jus
Adapted from "Perfect Prime Rib", *Cook's Illustrated*, November 1995
This and the other recipes below adapted from *Cook's Illustrated* are used with permission by Boston Common Press

Sautéed Pork Medallions in a Pan Sauce
Adapted from "The Way to Cook Pork Chops", *Cook's Illustrated*, September 1994

Barbecued Spare Ribs
Adapted from "Authentic Barbecued Ribs at Home", *Cook's Illustrated*, July 1994

Crab Cakes; Cold Mustard Sauce
The Simply Great Cookbook by Chuck Muer, Momentum Books (1992)
Reprinted with permission from Momentum Books, LLC

Creamed Spinach
Adapted from *Breakfast at Brennan's and Dinner Too* by Pip Brennan et al, Brennan's (1994)
Used with permission by Brennan's

Caesar Salad with Croutons
Adapted from "Caesar Salad Rediscovered", *Cook's Illustrated*, September 1997

978-0-595-37866-1
0-595-37866-8

Printed in the United States
49574LVS00005B/382-408

9 780595 378661